Preface

I am grateful to Stackpole Books for having the vision to want to republish this book. It is an important book, because of its subject, and it was a difficult book to write. People from all over the world wanted a say, and it became an immense task to decide how to sort through those many voices and how to concisely use so much information. The book could have been a three-volume encyclopedia. Thus a few of Royal's friends with whom I spoke may feel as though their contribution could have been more, and for that I apologize. A reader must sense that Royal had deep and involved experiences with many, which a book of any normal size can only suggest.

I am grateful that this book has been so well received. Five book reviews, for example, the only reviews of which I am aware, by Ed Webster, Jeff Achey, Rusty Baillie, Mick Ward, and Gurdon Miller, have confirmed the integrity and vision of both the subject and the work. The book also was the only American entry to be selected for the final short-list of the Tasker-Boardman Award in England, in 1993.

I know that this book is a very good one, despite a few rivals who have felt the urge to mildly discredit almost anything I write or who feel uneasy that I should be so complimentary to Royal. I would rather build people up than tear them down. I would rather look for the good and great in people as opposed to exploit and exaggerate the negative. I cannot worry about a few predictable jealousies among the climbing community, for my spirit of intent has always been an honest one: to write a book that pays long due tribute to a man who was the vision of those golden age climbs in Yosemite, a man who was the doer, prime mover, teacher, who invented so many techniques and held to such a high standard of ethics. Royal was simply magic and still is! He had and has the great charisma, something we can now, in retrospect, realize was spiritually based. Here is a man of honor and integrity -- a most worthy hero.

My goals also were to create a book that was of true literary quality and that Royal would feel good about. He is as honest as anyone I know and would not let me overly praise him or fall short in the writing department. He signed off on the book, with approval, as did another spiritually astute reader, Tom Frost. The only real criticism this book has gotten was that a few sentences of mine seemed to come as some kind of cosmic surprise, such as the first line of chapter II, "Life is full of virtual worlds that compel people to create them." A few reviewers did not like that sentence. But other readers appreciated it, and Frost said I would take the sentence out over his dead body. The only factual mistakes of which I know are in the last paragraph of page 27 and the first paragraph of page 28, whereas the date of the climbs mentioned is most likely 1960 instead of 1959. No one, including Royal, could sort out which date was actually correct. But both Royal and Tom Frost insist they met in early 1960, so those climbs mentioned must have been in 1960 instead of 1959. A footnote has been added to explain the discrepancy.

I have wondered what a less reverential approach to Royal Robbins would have yielded. But the austerities for one are the exaltations of another, and no biography has been painted but through the eyes of an author. Indeed this book is biased.

In the end, I am unpersuaded by any conclusion other than that of human growth. Royal's story is this: a path of progress. And such is what I have chosen as the focus of the book. Friends remember his touch of brooding menace, in the '60s, stern and troubling, and friends recall also his warm, mild, or genial moments. For Royal, there has been what the poet Reg Saner calls "a softening of rigidities" through the years. I have tried to make a study of Royal's spiritual evolution, as well as his development as a climber, and as a writer, businessman, husband, and father. His has been a full life's excitements, troubles, and revelations.

At the risk of autobiographical entry into biography, I have added to these pages impressions from my own involvement with Royal over the years--beginning in the book about halfway through. I offer these in the spirit of English writer Thom Gunn's "autobiographical biography" of the poet Yvor Winters, as a specific example of how Royal played for years in the souls of some of us, disturbing us, angering, or inspiring. I carefully weighed the choice to add a first-person viewpoint (where possible, I have moved myself left of center stage or refer to myself in third person). Certainly I am no more than one among Robbins' acquaintances and have no wish to hiddenly advertise the merits of our particular involvement.

My friend Tom Frost also gives a personal perspective--by way of his innumerable photos. I consider the book as much a Frost pictorial biography as an Ament literary one. Tom also read the manuscript and contributed countless insights.

The task of this book was greatly facilitated by the faith of Royal and Liz Robbins who opened their lives to me and offered useful critiques, ideas, and tales during the development of the text. They should probably be listed as co-authors, along with Beulah Chandler, Royal's mother. Beulah wrote many wonderful letters to me and provided anecdote after anecdote, pertaining

Royal Robbins

SPIRIT OF THE AGE

Pat Ament

For Sandra —
Congratulations —
you're a Guide!
First on the rope!

Royal Robbins

STACKPOLE
BOOKS

Published by
STACKPOLE BOOKS
5067 Ritter Road
Mechanicsburg, PA 17055

Printed in the United States

First edition

10   9   8   7   6   5   4   3   2

Previously published by Two Lights
10550 Quail St., Westminster, CO 80021

Cover design by Wendy Reynolds

Library of Congress Cataloging-in-Publication Data

Ament, Pat
   [Spirit of the Age]
   Royal Robbins: Spirit of the Age / Pat Ament.—1st ed.
       p. cm.
   Originally published: Spirit of the age. Lincoln, Neb.:
   Adventure's Meaning Press © 1992.
     Includes bibliographical references and index.
     ISBN 0-8117-2913-3
      1. Robbins, Royal. 2. Mountaineers—United States—Biography.
   3. Rock Climbing. I. Title.
   GV199.92.R62A54   1998
   796.52'23'092—dc21
   [B]   977-25724
                                          CIP

to Royal's childhood. She also supplied a wealth of letters Royal wrote to her faithfully year to year.

Reg Saner gave a considered, extremely helpful reaction to the text, as did Shannon Wade who judged it from the feminine as well as modern-climber point of view. John Gill gave these pages careful examination and offered beneficial wisdom, as did Dave Rearick. Ken Wilson offered helpful thoughts, as did TM Herbert, Joe Fitschen, Lito Tejada-Flores, and Chuck Pratt. Steve Roper helped with many details and facts.

This book was written with the input of various people, all who welcomed the project with great cooperation. I would like to express my appreciation to Tamara Robbins, Mark Brady, Kaitlin Klaussen, Layton Kor, Peter Croft, Jim Bridwell, Scott Titterington, Doug Tompkins, Mike O'Donnell, Glen Denny, Richard McCracken, John Cleare, Michael Chessler, Chris Bonington, Roger Brown, Richard DuMais, Harry Daley, Parley Hansen, Yvon Chouinard, Ralph Imbrogno, and Wendell and Margaret Ament. Finally I wish to thank Ed Serr for his many hours of assistance in the word-processing and layout of this project.

I am responsible for the research and selection of the photos in this book and am grateful to all who offered their photography freely. Apologies must be extended to any photographer we failed to credit, since we were uncertain who took a few of the older photos. We were unable to contact a few other individuals who took some of the photos among Royal's collection.

I would like to acknowledge and credit all of the various magazines that have published Royal's writings over the years. These publications are listed in the bibliography at the end of this book.

All of the cartoons in this book were done by Sheridan Anderson.

I hope this book will remain a testament of my, as well as Royal's, love for climbing, nature, and people. We share a sense of the sacredness of these experiences.

Pat Ament -- June 28, 1997

I dedicate this book to Tom Frost

1 El Capitan photo montage by Ken Wilson

"...teach me to run
where I need to, through straining
roots, among rock, my nerve-trees billowing up
in the unlocked animal blood
on fire with the genius of instinct."
    --Rod Taylor

I

In Yosemite in the spring of 1968, an American climber whose desire was greater than his fear started up the three thousand-foot wall of El Capitan alone.

This sort of undertaking epitomized Royal Robbins. It was an exploit unique in American mountaineering. Climbs had been soloed before. But no one had soloed a wall of El Cap's length or difficulty. Royal five years earlier had done the first solo of a big Yosemite wall, the thousand-foot overhang of the Leaning Tower in three-and-a-half storm-filled days.

After the seasoning of so many years of rock climbing, it was now less a question of whether he could succeed and more the inclination to set before himself another goal, one with more beauty or challenge, looking always to perfect the experience or to have the perfect experience, in some rare and fragile place of adventure. Where better than on the form of El Capitan? Here he could enjoy beauty as well as challenge. Just as an artist or a poet tries less for plot and more delicately to feel, Royal was attuned less to a summit than to the sheer splendor of El Capitan--its mysteries of light and its subtleties of shadow, the rock gorgeous, white, the enormous architectural cleavage, facets, folds, and sweeps of flawless granite rising with increasing steepness, every breeze in the forest below, every stream of the surroundings, animate.

He was continuing to perpetuate those qualities which to him were imaginatively sacred: freedom, courage, and awareness of the natural world, his intelligence polished to the texture of granite, to the beauty and soul-touching education of nature. This was a strong spirit at work.

He belayed himself, hammering pitons into cracks, running his rope through carabiners on pitons, a process where the hands would grasp and loosen and then grasp again, movements that evoked many memories of past years of climbing exploration.

While this adventure was a reflection of his hundreds and hundreds of climbs, it meant also life renewed--pure, passionate experience happening again in the apprehension, or the minor terror, of an immense wall of granite hovering far up into the sky. Climbers viewed his instincts as brilliant, his mind incisive. He had confidence in himself. Yet this was not a route where composure was easily maintained, and much of his consciousness was infused with struggle: the exacting piton placements, the repetitions of having to rappel down each section of rock to remove the gear placed, the wind keeping him cold and off balance, uneasy moments at the edge of falling, uncertainty whether or not the gear he was hanging from would hold, loneliness, no sense of camaraderie, days on the wall without conversation--except with himself.

Why had he gone alone? It was the insurgence of the instant. Perhaps he would find something of the Italian solo climber Walter Bonatti's achievements of the human spirit. Perhaps Royal would come away from the adventure stronger, or with more knowledge. He would see deeper into life. To solo was a sensation of independence--or rather total dependence upon oneself. He wanted to make a meaningful statement within this sphere of human activity. Royal wanted to do El Cap's first solo, but also he needed to explore his own thoughts and soul. He needed to measure himself in a new way against a familiar wall.

Royal Robbins was born at Point Pleasant, West Virginia, on February 3rd, 1935, to Royal Shannon and Beulah Robbins. His mother and father were in love but were very young. Royal's father, who went by the name of Shannon, felt he hadn't lived life yet. He became a bit of a womanizer. He was an aspiring writer, a minor-league baseball player, a hunter, was once the welterweight boxing champion of West Virginia, and was...difficult. Beulah divorced him in 1938. Royal felt--and would continue to feel into adulthood--that his father had left him, rather than that his mother and he departed from his father. Royal felt abandoned. He was three years old at the time.

Beulah married James Chandler, and they lived in Mansfield, Ohio, for three years. But James turned out to be alcoholic and violent. He physically and psychologically abused both Beulah and Royal and demanded that Royal change his name to Jimmy Chandler. Royal took this name. James became more violent and irrational. One night while in bed, Royal listened to an argument between his mother and stepfather. When he heard his mother say "Jim, put that knife down," he slipped out his bedroom window to seek help. When the police arrived, James escaped over the back fence.

Beulah eventually decided to get Jimmy (Royal) away from James and sent him to live with some religious friends who, unfortunately, also mistreated him. When Jimmy wet the bed, he was forced to stand under a cold shower and hold his face up into the flow of water. He nearly drowned.

The Chandlers moved to Los Angeles in 1941 and lived in Redondo Beach and then Hollywood. Beulah recalls that when Royal was in first grade he liked the ocean and climbed on the rocks of the breakwaters.

2 Royal on the way to Sunday School, Hollywood, California

She divorced James in '45 and moved in with his brother, Bill Chandler, and his wife, who also lived in the Los Angeles area. Bill made up in every way for his brother's deficiencies and was a good friend to Beulah. She braved her troubles and worked hard, first as a maid and then as cosmetics expert in a drugstore to try to make ends meet for her and Royal and to one day be able to afford a place that would be their own.

3 Royal, age 7

Now that they were free of James Chandler, Beulah had the notion to let Jimmy choose the name that he would go by. She recalls that Royal was "a little confused about everything, somewhat traumatized by the events of his life," but returning to his original name brought an instant change in him. Royal became a newfound person, as though he had discovered an important element of his identity that had been lost.

Beginning to be independent and self-sufficient at a young age, he sold papers on street corners, rain or shine, and worked as a janitor in a store. His mother worked all day. He washed his dishes, cooked his meals, and cleaned the kitchen. He bought his own clothes. He loved books. Beulah remembers, "Even when he was very young, I could give him a book. And he was happy just looking at the pages." Royal was shy and didn't talk much or relate well to other kids. This was in part because of what he had been through.

"He was very submissive," she recalls. Once when he needed a spanking, she simply asked him to lie across the bed. He did so, and she gave him a few swats. More than submissive, Royal trusted Beulah. She was gentle, and he was not the slightest bit afraid of her. She was, in fact, kind, caring, and had no interest in hurting him in any way. Her guidance came in the form of her positive attitudes, and Royal found her influence constant and consistent.

At age eleven or twelve, Royal made a trip to Detroit to see his real father. He found Shannon to be self-centered, eager to fight, and without warmth. Crossing a street together, a car pulled in front of them and stopped. Royal's father opened the back door of the car and walked through the back seat and out the opposite door. It was his way of saying to the people in the car that he did not appreciate their stopping in front of him, that he had no respect for them, and that HE was important. Royal wrote home about experiencing his first thunderstorm--a thrilling phenomenon he hadn't encountered in California. And with this trip to Detroit, he lost interest in ever seeing his father again.

Royal's father did change as years passed and later wrote and expressed sorrow over his mistakes. He was an intelligent man who loved adventure and the dangers of battling the elements. Shannon spent three years in Alaska during the war and for two years ran a tugboat in the Aleutian Islands. One night in a blinding snowstorm, the boat went onto a reef and split apart. The crew went down with it. Shannon broke his left shoulder and somehow was washed onto the shore of a little island. He lay there for three days before help reached him. He was from then on in one hospital after another and finally died in a veteran's hospital in Detroit at the age of fifty-four. Royal was given the news while on a climbing stay in Yosemite and did not go to the funeral.

Shortly after his visit to Detroit to see his father, Royal and a friend stole some hubcaps. The parents of the other boy stated to the judge that they had given up and could no longer be of any help to their son, but Royal's mother expressed her support for Royal and her belief in him. Royal was released to his mother. The other boy went to a juvenile facility and years later committed suicide. Although Royal could not resolve the feeling of being abandoned by his father, it weighed little compared to the strength he gained from his mother's faith.

Royal was unlike other kids, having already built much of his character out of hardship. He disliked T.V. and loved classical music. Royal's half sister Penny, born to James and Beulah, was often told to turn the T.V. off so that Royal could listen to his music. When she was six years old and he was twelve, Royal took Penny and their cousins to Griffith Park, in Los Angeles, where he showed them how to climb the rocks in the area.

At twelve or thirteen, Royal was honored in scouting, selected as the "Outdoor Scout" to represent Troop 127, called "the Rainbow Troop." A photo was taken of him shaking hands with the Los Angeles police commissioner, who co-sponsored the troop with scoutmaster Phil Bailey. Royal won a trip to the

6

High Sierra for two weeks. On that trip, members of the group succeeded at a roped ascent of Fin Dome--a peak near the Rae Lakes. During the climb, he found himself easily doing what the others thought was difficult--a harbinger of things to come. That trip opened Royal's eyes to the beauty of the Sierra.

4 Outdoor Scout

The troop had high aspirations and decided to raise money for a used Greyhound bus to travel across the United States to a Scout Jamboree. They made this money by selling pinion nuts door to door for months! On the trip, they stopped in the Badlands of South Dakota where Royal led several companion scouts down into some steep, narrow canyons. He bloodied his arm in a minor fall. When they returned, scoutmaster Bailey was displeased. He would later acknowledge that this was typical of Royal to be attracted to adventure and to lead others to follow him into it.

When Royal moved to a different part of Los Angeles, he joined a new troop that was less spit-and-polish and more into adventure. This was very agreeable to him, of course, and he was soon again involved in climbing mountains. The troop set off to make its third attempt of the eight thousand-foot North Face of Mount San Jacinto, which involved real rock climbing. On a prior attempt of the mountain, one of the scouts had broken his leg. An epic rescue had been required to get him out. But they were successful this time and reached the top in two days. Royal was up to his old tricks and was reprimanded for soloing a rock face by their camp without a rope. The scoutmaster, Al Wilkes, later conceded that "Probably Royal was the safest person on the mountain." Both Wilkes and Bailey partly took the place of the father Royal never had. He viewed them as remarkable men.

At fifteen, he found himself browsing through a book about mountaineering--called "High Conquest"--by James Ramsey Ullman. Royal turned to a picture of a steep rock wall where a man was clinging by fingers and toes. A rope tied to the climber's waist disappeared into space below. Royal was struck by the sense of commitment and by the confidence the climber exuded. The idea of mastering a perilous face of rock with skill and courage insistently appealed to Royal. At that moment, he had a vision of his destiny.

He and a friend filched a rope from a trucking company and visited the sandstone rocks of Stony Point in the San Fernando Valley, north of Los Angeles. Royal climbed with school friends at Bee Rock, Stony Point, and other rocks in the Los Angeles area. It was his mother's opinion that "He climbed in part to find his identity."

In the summer of 1951, at age fifteen, he and a couple of friends hitchhiked to Yosemite with cans of food in their packs and a few pitons. They camped for four days and tried to climb. They walked right up to the steep, glacier-polished granite, with comparative, if not prophetic, confidence, but discovered that they were not yet skilled enough to make much progress at anything. In fact, they couldn't get off the ground. Later, someone recommended that they try the climbing found along a trail above Glacier Point. They eagerly hiked up and located a small face of rock that in fact allowed them to enjoy a few short, successful ascents.

5 Royal, 15, liebacks a crack in the San Fernando Valley

In a school essay, entitled "What I Did Last Summer," he wrote of weekend climbing, going sometimes with friends and sometimes with the rock climbing section of the California Sierra Club. In the essay, he explained that when he was with the Sierra Club he usually climbed on rock in southern California but that over Labor Day (September '51) they ascended Mount Williamson--the second highest mountain in California.

6 Piton at Mt. Pacifico, Royal, 16, on Sierra Club trip

7 Rappel at Mt. Pacifico

8 Contemplating success

Royal went up a rock one day at Stony Point, hammered a piton into a crack, leaned back, and the piton pulled out. He fell twenty-five feet, landing in a pile of boulders. This could have been a premature end to the precocious Royal Robbins, except that miraculously he only broke an arm and sprained an ankle. Many years later, he would reflect that the advice of an instruction book on climbing was going through his head, telling him--without elaboration--to hammer in a piton and trust it. "The words of a book were guiding my actions," he noted, "instead of inner judgment." It was the folly of the young, and he was preserved--as though life had something greater in store for him. In two weeks, he was climbing again.

Royal and his friends looked for excitement in ways other than climbing. They started riding freight trains out of Los Angeles, catching boxcars for a few blocks at first. When they realized that they weren't getting caught or hurt, they took longer trips--such as into the Mojave desert, followed by a hitchhike home. They were always pushing it, in a spirit of fun and good adventure. They climbed all over the boxcars while the trains were in motion and prided themselves in jumps from one car to another. After mastering a jump, say from the top of a boxcar into a coal car, they went for a more difficult one. The big test came when Royal flew from the top of a boxcar moving in one direction to the top of a boxcar that was going in an opposite direction. Misjudging the speed of the trains, he gashed one of his hands as he flew onto the steel. But no matter, the feat had been accomplished. Feeling lucky, he also thought, "I'll never do that again."

At age 16, Royal quit high school while in the tenth grade. He felt the urge to take action in his life. He hated school, felt that he was learning nothing. He wasn't good at anything and wanted to excel at something. He wanted to do something "great." He went to work in the winter at a ski area in the San Gabriel Mountains of southern California, with the plan that he would work part-time jobs in summer.

That year, he returned to Yosemite and, in participation in a climb with the Sierra Club, ascended the regular route on the huge, imposing, Higher Cathedral Spire. He'd been told a little of the route, that it started by going up the wall as high as possible until a traverse could be made left. Royal accidentally led much higher than the normal traverse point and moved up difficult, unclimbed rock. People later called it "the Robbins Variation." Roy Gorin wrote in the summit register, "Definitely not recommended." It was evident that this young person was in possession of a great deal of talent.

His second year skiing, Royal was chosen as one of ten skiers to represent California in the Junior National Championships held in Brighton, Utah. He also began to excel at difficult, short bouldering problems at Stony Point and engaged in instinctive competitions with other climbers.

In 1950, '51, and '52, at Tahquitz Rock, in the mountains of southern California near Idylwild, he began to realize more and more that climbing was what he wanted to do. His first sight of Tahquitz revealed a distant, mysterious citadel of gray-white granite shrouded in blue air. The morning was slightly cold, and the feeling of impending adventure was all-pervading.

He became acquainted with John Mendenhall and Chuck Wilts with whom he spent time at Tahquitz. They were mentors, Royal recalls, "genuine individuals who genuinely loved climbing and who genuinely wanted to share it. They were free spirits from whom I learned attitudes and values."

Rock climbing was no longer a sidelight of Royal's life, rather a characteristic. He became the outstanding young climber of southern California and, in 1952, in the company of Don Wilson, did something exceptional at Tahquitz. A classic, three hundred-foot inside corner of rock called the "Open Book" had been led in 1947 by Mendenhall, with the use of wooden pitons and several pitons required for direct support of body weight. Royal led the climb without that "artificial" support known in climbing as "direct-aid." He had no tension from the rope or any piton. It was a first "free" ascent, later called the first climb in the country with a difficulty rating of 5.9. The level of 5.9 was, at that time, the top of the California climbers' decimal grading system. The ascent was a notable achievement, even more so because Royal was only seventeen. It was also an influential achievement. This free ascent marked a change in attitude for climbers throughout the country. The psychological barrier had been broken, and climbers everywhere soon were attempting similar "free ascents"--beginning to seriously attempt to climb without the use of direct-aid.

9 Royal, age 17, after East Buttress of Mt. Whitney

In 1953, as a somewhat self-assured climber at the age of eighteen, Royal teamed with Jerry Gallwas and Don Wilson to make the second ascent of the exalted, seventeen hundred-foot, Salathe-Steck route on the North Face of Sentinel Rock in Yosemite. The first ascent three years earlier had taken four and a half gruelling days. Prepared for five days on the wall, Royal and his friends were infused with energy and made it in a little less than two days. Royal was wearing tennis shoes.

With only sweaters for warmth, the three spent the night sitting, shivering, on a ledge atop the Flying Buttress halfway up the wall. They didn't mind the cold, because "it was adventure."

10 The North Face of Sentinel Rock (West Face in sunlight)-- photo by Harry Daley

At one point on the second day of the climb, Royal lowered his friends to where they could traverse and then ascend to a position above him. When his turn came to swing across the rock by the rope, which was now attached above, he naively thought he would be able to hold the rope and simply walk across the wall. He lost control and swung about a hundred and fifty feet. When he finally stopped, he was battered and surprised. He would later reflect in an interview, "We were young and healthy and resilient, and it was O.K."

Higher on the wall, at a notable place where the original route moved outward and up a tremendously exposed face with the use of direct-aid and the drilling of several expansion bolts, Royal pioneered a free-climbing alternative. Deep within the crack, and above their heads, was a hidden passage Royal was grateful to hide in and try to follow upward to some hopeful exit. Going outside and along the Salathe-Steck route, up the airy face, was not something to which Royal or his friends were constitutionally inclined. Out there, hundreds of feet of rock swept downward in one scary drop. Rather than that, he was happy to try to crawl up this long, dark, claustrophobic passage and find where it led. It seemed better to become stuck inside this night-like place, squeezed between two plates of rock, than petrified outside.

Wiggling up by inches, Royal found a miraculous exit at the top of the passage that joined the other route where there was less exposure. This variation, later named "the Narrows," would come to be thought of by climbers with equal fear to Salathe's exposed wall. The choices were: a void of mind-exploding space below or the panic of an endless, lung-crushing enclosure.

Such instances of ingenuity in leading were recognized by the climbing community of Yosemite and California--not altogether without resentment from the "old guard" of climbers, including a few members of the Sierra Club. Fate had unleashed Royal Robbins upon the scene, a maverick kid who was creating adventure and who was blitzing people's mentality of what was climbable.

He made the third ascent of the Salathe-Steck on Sentinel within the year, this time with Mike Sherrick--in Royal's words, "a joyful character, generous spirited, one who said good things about others, who enjoyed life, and who was unusually talented--certainly more so than myself--in climbing." Friendship was not incidental to climbing but was added reason to explore the rare, ethereal heights of Yosemite. Besides the building of individuality, there occurred the cooperative aspect of climbing's ever-seeming, dazzling art.

Royal and Sherrick reduced the time that had been required on Royal's previous ascent, making the summit in a little over a day.

On another Sierra Club climb, Royal met Joe Fitschen whose personality and love of climbing blended well with Royal's. Fitschen recalls, "When I met

Royal, he was climbing with Don Wilson. We became friends. Neither of us had a car. We'd get one of our mothers to drive us to the L.A. bus station, and we'd head north to one of the climbing areas. I don't remember how we got home."

Royal worked for a few years as a bookkeeper at Union Bank in Los Angeles. The bank was an environment incongruous with the airy, spirited adventures of ascending rock. But until the clearer meaning (as to who he was) did begin to crystallize, the bank satisfied the need for a job. While working at the bank, he attended night school and earned his high school diploma.

11 Royal (left) at the bank

On another climb at Tahquitz Rock, Royal's partner Warren Harding--with whom Royal would later develop a famous rivalry--had arranged a "hanging belay" from two questionably placed pitons. The worst-looking of the two pitons was a small, wafer-like strip of soft iron driven upward into a crack. As Royal arrived at the belay, the other piton pulled out. Both climbers were dangling suddenly from that lone, tiny, dubiously wedged spoon of metal in a crack. "Let's get some hardware in," Royal is said to have stated earnestly, and they did, and they survived.

Despite such dire moments, climbing was, for Royal, exaltation. It spoke to him of "man's struggle against his own fears and weaknesses." He was drawn by what the rock symbolized, by "the purity of the ideal."

II

Life is full of virtual worlds that compel people to create them.

In 1955, a lavish and spectacular idea appeared on the horizon: that a climb might be done up the Northwest Face of Half Dome--the great rock sitting high at the east shoulder of Yosemite. The Northwest Face, a flat, vertical surface two thousand feet high and more than two thousand feet wide, was pink or sometimes gold in afternoon sun. Facing slightly west, it stood as a dominating sight from the floor of the Valley. Except for El Capitan, Half Dome was the most striking formation in Yosemite.

12 Half Dome in clouds -- photo by Tom Frost

At twenty, Royal was an experienced climber and intrigued by the possibility of such an adventure. He, Warren Harding, Jerry Gallwas, and Don

Wilson started up this overwhelming wilderness of granite. No one before had been on a wall of rock of such serious dimensions and requiring this degree of commitment. But after three days of climbing and only four hundred and fifty feet of progress, Jerry and Don began to have doubts as to their success. Royal and Warren were willing to pain their way onward for whatever necessary extra days might still be ahead, but the four finally decided to admit that things weren't right yet for the ascent. It was not defeat, rather delay, and they rappelled. A time would come to return to the wall.

Royal later portrayed Jerry and Don as "more balanced individuals," whereas he and Warren were "more passionate."

In the summer of '56, Royal managed a difficult free ascent of "the Innominate" on Tahquitz Rock. The crux, formerly requiring six pitons of direct-aid, was an open book "with both leaves of the book overhanging." TM Herbert recalls watching Royal lead this route:

"That was brilliant. Royal was so strong and determined. That was bad-ass climbing! Royal was in his high-top tennis shoes. When he came down from the climb, I asked why he didn't wear lug soles. He said he just happened to have his tennis shoes with him that weekend."

On September 1st of 1956, Mark Powell, Joe Fitschen, and Royal completed the first ascent of the South Face of Liberty Cap, after a day and a half of climbing. There were fourteen rope lengths, and Powell led the crux aid-pitch. In the *Sierra Club Bulletin* of June '57, Royal wrote, "Mark placed a tiny knife-blade piton." These very thin, small pitons were available to a few climbers, homemade by Chuck Wilts and later from the creative anvil of Yvon Chouinard. Although driven into the crack not more than a quarter of an inch, the knifeblade piton held Mark's weight and enabled them to succeed at the ascent without having to drill any holes in the rock for expansion bolts.

There were climbers in the country and in other places of the world who felt little aversion to bolting and who, in some cases, preferred bolting to risk. A few climbers were simply not creative enough to invent ways around or over difficult climbing problems without the use of bolts. In contrast, a different mentality was beginning to surface in American climbing: where bolts were to be avoided. Climbers of this philosophy felt that it was better to apply every creative resource before resorting to a bolt. This would become a theme of Royal's career, to use as few expansion bolts as possible.

In June of 1957, Royal invited Fitschen to join him, along with Jerry Gallwas, and Mike Sherrick, on another attempt of Half Dome. Fitschen's boss, however, wouldn't let him off. The climbers could wait no longer, nor could they wait for Harding who was in Alaska and not yet able to get to Yosemite.

Half Dome had occupied Royal's thoughts, and he, Jerry, and Mike were eager. Jerry brought along some homemade pitons he had newly forged. He was a good craftsman and made small work-of-art pitons specifically for Half Dome. He also made excellent bigger pitons, one to two-inches in width. These were patterned after John Salathe's own homemade, hard-steel pitons.

The edges of lug-soled boots were placed on small footholds. Hands were shaped to the rock, in places where holds could be found. Nylon rope was fed out to the leader from around the back of the belayer. The climbers hammered their small, steel pitons into cracks and clipped two loops of thin rope together as an aid-sling to attach to the pitons and stand in. Movement was made piton by piton, upward into the absolutely vertical expanse of granite. Techniques had to be invented, meager acts of faith, during the course of the ascent.

In part due to Royal's route-finding adeptness, they worked out a critical, connecting traverse across the wall to the right that took them to more promising cracks. The position of the climbers overlooked the depth of Yosemite, a feeling of tremendous height above the wonderful, noble, ponderosa and sugar pines. Along this open, giddy traverse hundreds of feet up, Royal was lowered down the wall by one of his companions and, with the rope running through a carabiner on a piton, pendulumed back and forth across the rock. After four attempts, he was able to cling to a handhold at the end of the swing.

The three friends had somewhat unceremoniously become climbers and had ventured upward, into the unknown, like children with pride in their magic. They were held in the spell of this vast wall, held by the mystery that hovered around Half Dome's form. Some kind of metaphysical sense of obligation was speaking to their psyche, an urgency, a feeling. An idea of rightness. An idea of the beauty of the rock. They were high up in the natural world: water dripping from the upper reaches of the wall, sunlight glancing across the foliated granite, rock running in vertical sheets with black edges, the rock grayish-blue, an aroma of lichen, clouds carrying the pinks of sun, a scent of red fir trees or of manzanita.

Near the top of the wall, far above, were huge overhangs that might be unclimbable. It was doubtful that a retreat would be possible from so high up the wall. There were no rescue services in Yosemite.

In the event that they should be turned back by the overhangs near the summit and would be forced to attempt a long series of rappels, they fixed one of their hundred-and-twenty-foot ropes on the traverse and left it hanging there as a means by which they might reverse the pendulum maneuvers. Later in the *Sierra Club Bulletin* of November 1958, they offered the following piece of information: "Let this serve as a warning to future parties: it (the fixed rope) is not fixed on the top." The reason for this lack of anchoring at the top was that they could not find a secure anchor without leaving at least two precious pitons. But also the adventure would be preserved for future climbing parties--who would not be allowed to enjoy the use of the rope to ascend!

13 Royal leading on Half Dome -- photo by Jerry Gallwas

14 Half Dome, a vertical climb of two thousand feet -- photo courtesy of the Department of Interior

Eventually the three climbers encountered "Psyche Flake," a wide, seventy-foot high, detached structure of granite sitting on a small ledge and clinging mysteriously--if not miraculously--to the wall. The flake was held there by no apparent means other than a point or two of contact with the main wall and a few wedged chockstones. It would be dangerous to fool with this hulk of imminently exfoliating granite. The climbers, nonetheless, went behind the flake and, exercising faith, ascended with backs against the main wall and feet pushing outward against the flake. They were not willing to be conquered by the thought-

-however alarming--that they might push the flake off and go sailing down with it into the infinity below. This flake disappeared of its own accord a few years later.

High on the "Zig-Zags" (vertical flakes that angled one direction and then another), the stillness of Half Dome was interrupted only as laughter resounded faintly or there occurred sounds of hammer against piton.

Just beneath the summit overhangs, they discovered a narrow "Thank God Ledge" that allowed them to walk and crawl to the left where less steep rock brought them to the top of the first Grade VI in America. It was the evening of the fifth day, and Harding--unable to return to Yosemite in time to be a part of the ascent--greeted them on the summit. Harding had hiked up the eight-mile trail that circles Half Dome to the south and had reached the top via the "cable route"--a scramble up the east flank of the rock.

Harding was disappointed that he was not a part of the ascent and, not to be outdone, would soon begin his own new project on an even greater wall: Yosemite's three thousand-foot South Buttress (Nose) of El Capitan.

The challenges Royal had to climb out of were not always on rock. His youthful virility manifested itself in a short, disastrous relationship with a Los Angeles woman, "Grace," who he had dated from time to time for about a year. Feeling a sense of "moral obligation," he drove with her to Las Vegas and on July 14, 1957, married her. Almost immediately, she became cold toward him. The marriage was insufficient to overcome the fact that the two were not in love. With her agreement, in early September, he left. Royal then learned of her history of promiscuity and that she was the mother of several children, and that she was still married to another man when he married her! She had played on Royal's integrity and, under strange pretexts, had lured him into this ill-conceived marriage. They parted ways, quickly, although it took a bit longer to sort out the equally freak legal embroilments. After much mental inconvenience to Royal, this footnote of his life was ended officially.

It was difficult for Royal to reconcile this misadventure, perhaps because of how reckless he had been, or naive, or how manipulated. He pushed the emotions of the affair away rather than deal anymore with them. The whole matter soon became like a dream to him, vague and very distant, as though it never really had happened.

At Tahquitz in late August of 1957, Royal and Fitschen met Dave Rearick, a calm, thoughtful person and an excellent climber. They invited Rearick to test himself on the Open Book, and Dave led the crux pitch. The three solo-downclimbed the Trough (5.0), a customary route of descent for Royal but which made Rearick a bit nervous. Below, they met John Mendenhall. The four now decided to try the Innominate. Rearick and Fitschen formed one roped team, Royal and Mendenhall another.

Rearick had heard quite a lot about the climbing of Robbins and was inspired to have Royal now with him, coming up under his heels. At the crux overhanging dihedral, Rearick suddenly saw the sequence and did it. TM Herbert and other friends were at the bottom, cheering Dave on. Royal was impressed by how well Dave did the climb. Rearick describes these events as "the most memorable day of my life." A few hours later, Royal invited Rearick to go to Yosemite with him.

15 Rearick starts up the Innominate -- photo by Gordon Oates

In a week, Royal, Fitschen, and Rearick were in Yosemite, standing below the Lost Arrow Chimney--a fissure rising twelve hundred feet up the great wall east of Yosemite Falls. The chimney had been climbed in 1947 in five days by John Salathe and Anton Nelson and was the first "big-wall" climb in Yosemite, a bold, difficult one. Only two more ascents of it had been managed in the ten years since its first ascent. Royal decided that two people could do the route in faster time, so over Labor Day weekend, September 1957, he and Fitschen made the wall's fourth ascent--with a time on the route of only two days.

When Fitschen volunteered for the army, Royal told him how absurd it was to do such a thing. Four days later, Royal received his draft notice. They laughed and, by a happy stroke of fate, were sent to the same basic-training barracks at Fort Ord in Monterey from where, on weekend leaves, they could hitchhike about, play, and climb.

Royal wrote letters regularly to his mother:

"March 22, Fort Ord.
Dear Mother,
Well I'm here, and I hate it. Two years! I'll be dead when I get out.... They put me in charge of all the men (62), and I was responsible for them from the induction center to Monterey. I guess they picked me because of my moderately high score on the mental test.... Some of my fellows seem like pretty agreeable people, but I don't mix much and stay pretty much apart, quiet and observing.... I have been eating a lot, though the food here is very bad. I'd better watch it, or it'll bother my climbing--getting heavy that is...."

"March 31, 1958,
Dear Mother,
Things have already begun to get a bit tougher and will certainly get much worse, but I'm adapting fairly well and getting along just fine.... Some of the sergeants here are OK, but many of them are just stupid asses.... A bright spot is that Joe, the fellow with the butch who used to come over quite often, is here in the same barracks as I, though not in the same platoon. Most of the fellows here are pretty much at a loss when confined to barracks. They have nothing to do. But I have no problems; I'm either reading, writing, or playing chess, and never bored.... We've had either rain or considerable cloudiness every day since I got here.... The country is rather interesting--gently rolling hills for 10 or 15 miles to where steeper country begins, and the ocean to the west. The hills are covered with a combination of green grass and small, shrub-like trees and are rather pretty this time of year...."

"April 7, 1958,
Dear Mother,
Army life isn't too bad--I'm in good shape, so the physical exertion doesn't bother me.... It's 9:30 p.m. now--lights are out at 9:15 p.m. And so I'm writing this in the latrine, sitting on the floor (which is clean) next to the heater. We must be in bed by ten and then up again at 5:30 a.m.--a very vigorous and healthy life and one to which I am well suited, being strong, energetic, and always driving myself anyway. But I don't want to be a soldier. Though I realize of course that the country must be defended in time of need, and I'm obliged to be ready to do so...."

"April 19, 1958,
Dear Mother,
I've been bothered by a cold which has caused me to fatigue easily, so I haven't had the energy to stay up late and write letters.... Starting today I am sleeping in a separate little room with three other fellows. The reason for this is that the sergeant, exasperated by the inefficiency of our squad leader, has appointed me to take his place. So I am now the leader of the 4th squad. This means I'll be responsible for about thirteen fellows. Our squad is one of four which make up our platoon, the 4th, which is one of five platoons which make up our company, namely Co. A. Follow me? At any rate, I am now in a more interesting position which has certain advantages, such as less manual labor, etc. Of course, if I don't do my job well I'll be kicked out too. However, I probably don't have too much to worry about.... Even today the lieutenant, after I had answered a couple of military questions precisely at inspection, told me he thought I was a very good soldier. Me! Of all people! I was rather surprised and a little depressed when he said this. I don't feel particularly honored that he thought I was living up to his idea of a 'good soldier.' Ah well...."

"May 5, 1958,
Dear Mother,
The army will probably make me a clerk-typist.... I was given the opportunity to attend Officer Candidate School but let it pass. I can't really believe in the principles and ideals of the army and would suffer if I were in a position where I had to make it appear that I did believe in them.... My hair is again growing out. I no longer look like such a cue-ball convict, but you'd still be shocked to see me...."

"June 23, 1958,
Dear Mother,

I'm sitting in an on-post cafe, relaxing and drinking beer with some friends. We have classes from 8 to 5 each day, and our time is pretty much our own after that.... We average about three hours of typing a day and spend the rest of the time being lectured to about various army clerical set-ups.... In the test we had last Friday which covered what we had been taught the first week, guess who got the highest score in the class? So, mother dear, things are no longer so rough as they were in basic training, but oh boy do I miss my freedom! The freedom to move around and do what I please means so much to me.... I spent last weekend very happily in San Francisco. I love that place. The people there are so warm and human. The city seems so filled with love and human warm-heartedness.... A ride on a San Francisco trolley or cable car is quite an experience after Los Angeles busses. I spent Saturday night wandering in the bohemian section, which is the best part of the city. I went from bar to cabaret to coffee house and enjoyed myself considerably. Having drunk a bit of beer and wine, I was feeling quite jovial...."

"July 6, 1958,
Dear Mother,
...Ol' scholar Robbins is still doing well in his school work. Out of the three tests we've had so far, I got one perfect score and two 98's. It is not that I think the work is worth the effort--it definitely is not. But you know me, always an extremist, always all out; and since I have to go through this crap, I figure I might as well do it up right.... I spent last weekend in San Francisco and really had a great time. Joe (Fitschen) and John Field and I were together. Money was scarce, and we resorted to various fantastic devices for saving it. For example, John got a room for a dollar and a quarter a night and Joe and I came in through the window, and we slept two on the bed and one on the floor. Also, most of my food for the three-day weekend consisted of loaves of rye bread...."

Royal and Fitschen separated at the end of basic-training, and Royal was stationed at Fort Bliss, Texas, where he served as a clerk in Officers' Records. During this time, he frequently forged passes and caught military airplane rides to California in order to climb on weekends at Tahquitz Rock and in Yosemite. Hitchhiking and freight trains were other means of transport to get to California for a couple of days of climbing. He would arrive back at Fort Bliss on Sundays or occasionally on Monday mornings with only enough leeway to shave, change clothes, and report to work. Over one period, he made it to California on ten straight weekends.

A letter to his mother from Fort Bliss, dated September 5, 1958, describes a few of the happenings on one of these weekend trips to California:

"Dear Mother,

Friday night I left the post here and went over to the airport a couple miles away to see if I could catch a military plane to the West Coast. Things looked good at first, and I thought I had a ride to San Bernardino. However, through a misunderstanding and wrong information, I missed the plane and had to wait there all night to catch a 'hap' to Oakland next morning at 8:00. We arrived at Oakland at 2:30 p.m., and I immediately (a bit of luck!) caught a flight to San Diego, from where I hitchhiked to LA, arriving home about 10:00. I listened to a few records, drank a little beer, ate some macaroni Penny fixed for me, and went to bed, determined to get up early and make the most of Sunday.

"After eating a large breakfast Sunday morning, I dropped by Jerry's house and then took off for West LA to see Lin Ephraim. He wasn't home, so I drove south to San Onofre (about 50 miles), arriving about 3:00 in the afternoon. San Onofre is a beach area where lots of skiers and surfers gather. I met some friends who loaned me a surfboard and invited me to dinner. Everybody had to leave about 10:00 pm.

"I walked up to the car to drive home, already feeling I had stayed longer than was wise. As I started to drive off, I noticed the car felt funny. Getting out, I found there was a flat in the right rear tire. Then I opened the trunk and couldn't find the lug-wrench. It was three miles to the nearest gas station, and believe me after walking that distance and getting back and finding out that the jack didn't work--I was really ready to flip. Anyway, after working on that infernal jack for an hour, I realized I would have to get going if I was going to get--to the post on time. So, as there seemed to be nothing else to do, I drove the car to the gas station. I think this probably ruined the tire; you'd better have it checked. As usual, all I can say is I'm sorry to be causing you more trouble and expense....

"Anyway, I got home about 5:00 in the morning and almost immediately started thumbing my way back here. A man soon picked me up and, professing to know the road, took me 30 miles out of my way. After this late start, I had trouble getting a ride but finally made my way to a place near Palm Springs where a very easy-going couple with their small son picked me up and said they would take me to Desert Center, about 45 miles from Blythe.

"We finally got there, but not before having a blowout and having to change a tire in 105 degree heat. My next ride was with a man in a truck carrying several airplane engines and bound for Phoenix, Arizona, which was about half the total distance and would leave me with about 400 miles to go. However, before he had driven very far, the tread on one of his tires began to come off and we had to drive about 40 mph for over a hundred miles.

"Arriving in Phoenix at twilight, three rides were required just to get me across that huge, monstrously spread out city. Things at this time looked bad, and my hopes were low. I realized that if I was going to make it back on time I'd have to catch a ride going all the way, and this was unlikely. However, believe it or not, it happened. Two soldiers destined for Fort Bliss picked me up and brought me right to my barracks...."

Royal was impressed with one superior at Fort Bliss, Officer Ryerson, "an enlightened and compassionate leader who nevertheless challenged me to excel in my duties."

Royal convinced his senior officers at Fort Bliss to give him a thousand dollars and a month's leave to try out for the Olympics in skiing. This was slightly stretching the truth about his abilities, and Royal knew it, but it was a good way to get free for awhile. At Squaw Valley, he never really did try out for the Olympics. Instead, he ended up in Reno, Nevada, and, with seven hundred dollars remaining, decided to try his hand at gambling. He surprised himself with an impressive run of luck, upon which the management started awarding him with drinks along with his winnings. He soon lost everything, including the entire seven hundred dollars. He phoned Fitschen for a loan and continued along his journey. Stopping at the University of Utah in Salt Lake City, he studied at the university library and spent time sitting in the cafeteria.

June 15, 1959, while on a short furlough from the army, Royal and Dave Rearick climbed "the Vampire" at Tahquitz, an outstanding and spectacular first ascent. In the small newsletter *Mugelnoos*, published by the Sierra Club, Royal wrote of the Vampire: "This climb is exceptionally interesting and, considering its appalling appearance, remarkably reasonable. We considered calling it the 'Flakety Flakes,' because it appeared flakier than the Flakes. But this is almost plagiarism, so we named it the 'Vampire,' to connote that it has something in common with the Bat, but is greater and more bloodsucking."

In August of '59, Royal--whose address still was Fort Bliss, Texas, but who continued to find ways to make weekend appearances in Yosemite--made the eighth ascent of Sentinel Rock with Pete Rogowski and Lin Ephraim (with Frost and Fitschen on a separate rope close by, doing the same route). Royal, Frost, and Fitschen also climbed the continuously difficult East Bridalveil Falls route in six hours and had a swim and lunch on top.

Editor's Note: The Sentinel Climb and East Bridalveil Falls climb mentioned in the previous paragraph, and the Crack of Dawn climb mentioned in the first paragraph of the next page were most likely done in 1960 rather than 1959. There were a number of conflicting sources, but both Royal and Tom Frost insist they met in about February of 1960 at Tahquitz Rock. Thus the above mentioned climbs must have taken place in the summer after that, or else Royal and Tom met in 1959 instead of 1960. The mystery remains unsolved.

16 Bridalveil Creek at low water, good for swimming -- photo by Richard McCracken

Royal climbed the "Crack of Dawn" with Frost and Chuck Pratt. Their idea here was to establish a new route that would be separate and distinct from the classic Arches route. They were eventually forced to join the Arches route in the vicinity of the "Rotten Log" and managed to by-pass the log without using it.

In this period, Fitschen and Royal made the second ascent of the North Face of Middle Cathedral Rock. Pratt, Steve Roper, and Bob Kamps had made the route's first ascent two months earlier. In the October 1959 *Mugelnoos*, Royal wrote of Middle Cathedral:

"The climb was completed in two days, with the night passed fairly comfortably about fifty feet above the Pratt Chimney. Chuck's lead of this chimney is certainly one of the most remarkable leads in the history of American mountain climbing.... Two pitches from the top, we were struck by a terrific rainstorm. 'It's OK, Joe,' I said, 'They're cumulus clouds, just intermittent showers.' An hour later, as the rain continued to pour, and the lightning to flash, and the thunder to roll (with TM Herbert yodeling from the Valley, sounding like Tarzan calling for Tantor), we decided (soaked through and chilled) we had better make a try for the top.... The last pitch was a slimy, delicate, and 'spooky' chimney, and we arrived on top just as the rain ceased, an hour before nightfall. Five hours later, after a phantasmagoria of bushwhacking, slippery lichen, loose rock, and hung-up rappels, we were motoring...through the most wizard combination of fog, cloud, moon, and mountain solemnity to be imagined."

When Royal's term in the army ended, he moved to Berkeley, California, and took a job at the Berkeley branch of the American Trust Company where he earned three hundred and fifty dollars a month. He stayed in Berkeley with Krehe Ritter, Charlie Raymond, Lito Tejada-Flores, and Dick McCracken. It was a "pad" frequented by other friends who were in Berkeley, including Janie Taylor and Joe Fitschen, also Chuck Pratt--one of the leading lights of the University of California hiking club.

In a climbing article, Royal wrote about the Berkeley residence: "We could play Brahms at ear-splitting levels, sing and shout, folk dance, eat cheese and bread, and down jugs of wine." They also read and played chess. The point wasn't luxury, it was freedom.

17 Chuck Pratt -- photo by Royal Robbins

Lito Tejada-Flores remembers: "At Krehe's, it was a classic 'college-kid' life. Joe Fitschen was a jazz musician (trombone). Krehe also was a musician. We had raging discussions late into the night, about Bertrand Russell, or someone. Royal had gone into areas of thought that were deeper than ours, a real autodidact, self-taught. He had not gone to college and been badgered by professors to read. He did it on his own. I viewed him as a rock climber. It seemed strange that he worked in a bank--going to work and doing what regular people do. We would all wander up to Indian Rock, a boulder in the middle of the town of Berkeley, and climb. At folk dancing, something some of us did, Royal was not coordinated. It was a puzzle to me how this person with two left feet at dancing could be so good at climbing. At Indian Rock, Royal would be hanging on these little mantel shelves and small holds, crimping his wrists and fingers, standing on tiny things a foot above the ground, and would go way past the limits of endurance to stay on the rock. He put the same intensity into these boulder problems as one would if he were high off the ground and couldn't risk a fall. He was really fierce."

Royal had, by this time, developed a remarkable network of lasting friendships, a group of individuals who in their own right would make profound contributions to climbing and who would achieve heights in their own lives.

TM Herbert, a humorist of astounding spontaneity, was one such friend. At a restaurant on the way to Tahquitz Rock, with Rearick and Royal and others, TM was so funny, Royal recalls, "that we were actually falling out of our chairs." TM challenged the others to describe what they saw in a scoop of ice cream floating in root beer. TM's own answer was "a bald-headed man standing on his tiptoes in quicksand." TM had a wonderful ability to produce things out of his imagination with superb timing, regaling his friends around campfires or while they were trying to concentrate on a difficult climbing move.

As a bank teller, Royal was more quiet, less conversant, than other tellers. It was not his forte to try to make people feel comfortable or to tire them with commentaries about the weather or the world's worries. His thoughts were more with climbing, and he was sociable within his climbing circle.

After a few months at the bank, he decided to devote himself to what he loved. He quit the bank, saying in essence, "Goodbye, I'm going climbing." It was at this point that he departed on the Road Less Traveled and never turned back toward a regular, work-a-day life.

At this same time, Tom Frost--an aeronautical engineer who had taken up climbing--searched out the rock climbing section of the Sierra Club. He started going to Stony Point, Tahquitz Rock, and Mount Pacifico--an area just

18 TM Herbert, Yosemite, all smiles, head as big as boulder

north of Los Angeles in the San Gabriel Mountains. His companions, a lighthearted group, consisted of TM Herbert, Yvon Chouinard, Harry Daley, Don Lauria, Tom Condon, and Joe Fitschen--who particularly was recognized as a friend of Royal's. In the company of these people, several of whom referred to themselves as the BRC (Bachelor Rock Climbers), Frost heard frequent mention of Robbins. According to Frost, "It was with an aura of mystery and reverence that Royal's name was used."

Then one January or February day of 1960, while climbing on the 20-foot cliffs of Mount Pacifico, someone showed Frost a diagonal finger-crack up rock so steep that it was slightly overhung, a route called "the Robbins Eliminate." The climbs Royal did seemed to evoke a spirit of awe. Frost returned to Los Angeles, trained, dieted, and focused his thoughts for a month on the Robbins Eliminate. When he came back to the route, Royal happened to be there. Frost climbed the route. Robbins was sitting on a rock and observed the ascent. He said very little, other than a quiet "Nice going"--a valuable note of approval from the mysterious prodigy-climber and enough to serve as the beginning of a friendship.

A month or so later, in May, 1960, Frost led the first free ascent of "Dave's Deviation" at Tahquitz, a steep, smooth seam near the bottom of the rock. Royal was there again and was pleased with Frost's effort. He took occasion to walk down the trail with Tom and spoke of his desire to repeat Harding's climb of El Capitan (the Nose) in the near future. The information was offered in the sense of an invitation, and Frost--largely unaware of what he was getting himself into--was more than happy to be a part of the plan.

But first, Royal wanted to push the line of Dave's Deviation all the way up Tahquitz Rock. He soon teamed with Frost to complete the first ascent of those upper pitches of the route. It was one of the first climbs approaching a grade of 5.10 in the country. Only a climber by the name of John Gill had mastered this level of difficulty, solo on buttresses of the Grand Tetons in Wyoming and on spires in the Needles of South Dakota.

In the same year, Frost also led "The Blank," another Tahquitz 5.10. This capable, humble, and most genial of climbers was to become a cherished partner of Royal's for years to come.

19 L. to R.: Harry Daley, Tom Frost, Royal Robbins, Yvon Chouinard, at Stony Point -- photo by Roger Brown

20 Royal doing a "no-hands" ascent at Stony Point -- photo by Roger Brown

Royal next ascended the North Face of Lower Cathedral Rock in Yosemite, with Pratt and Joe Fitschen. From June 2nd until noon June 4th, they struggled on this fifteen hundred-foot wall. Chuck was not only good in cracks but also at aid-climbing and, to get over an especially troublesome section of rock, placed six successive knife-blade pitons. One of these pulled out as Royal followed the pitch, and three of the pitons came out under Joe's weight. With its loose, unpleasant rock and dangerous problems, the climb was as severe as any Royal had done.

Royal led Rearick up the East Chimney of Rixon's Pinnacle in June 1960. This crack, located a short walk through the forest west of their campsite in Yosemite, was a significant climbing feat. Formed by a huge block of rock leaning upward at a right-slant against another wall, the crack tended to drop a person out of it. Due to a slab of granite filling the inside of the crack, there were only a few inches of depth to the crack for the few feet it overhung most. The edges of the crack were rounded, with no easy way of getting any part of the body to jam inside. This intense, backward-leaning, "off-width" crack called forth the highest mastery of free-climbing: a strenuous combination of techniques, pushing and pulling, pressing with knees and elbows in opposition, feet attempting to bridge the crack with odd, twisting, heel-toe wedges, and a slippery "lieback." Rearick recalls that Royal first started up a steep crack to the left, placed a piton, and liebacked up to where he took a long fall. Royal was fortunately caught by the rope through the piton just before hitting the ground. He brushed himself off and moved to the crack to the right.

The East Chimney of Rixon's was rated 5.9 by Royal but was decidedly more difficult than that. Years later, people recognized that this was the first 5.10 route in Yosemite (predating the commonly-thought first 5.10: Pratt's "Crack of Doom").

In late June of '60, Royal and Rearick made the third ascent of the Northwest Face of Half Dome. Frost, Pratt, and Fitschen, had done the second ascent of this great plaque of rock a week or so earlier and required only two and one-third days. "Royal was anxious to do it in two days," Rearick recalls. "These were big adventures, and a three-man team was considered safer and stronger. But Royal decided that just the two of us would do it." Royal and Rearick took only two days, and Rearick would carry with him for many years a sense of the fear he experienced at the dangerous, loose-looking Psyche Flake. He recollects being able to see out through the bottom of the flake, down into the distressing emptiness below. As Royal climbed, pushing with his feet straight out against the flake, he consoled Rearick (and himself) with the words, "Think of the hundreds of years of ice that have been pressing against this flake. No two mere mortals are going to disturb its presence."

When a climbing party a few years later discovered that Psyche Flake was missing, people hoped that an ascent was not being made of the flake at the time of its (and whoever's) cataclysmic demise.

"As he thinketh in his heart, so is he" (Proverbs 23:7).

Still pushing his vision up into the majestic granite walls of Yosemite, Royal pioneered the Royal Arches Direct with partner Joe Fitschen. The climb took three days, from June 24 to 26 of 1960, with summer heat becoming intense. The cracks were dirty, and one lead took Royal ten hours. He fell three times on that single pitch, the longest fall going fifty feet. It was the most formidable direct-aid problem he had ever encountered.

A sense of the affinity between Robbins and Fitschen is felt in a short retrospective of Fitschen offered by Royal: "A nice guy through and through, a good friend, an engaging conversationalist of the liberal bent with whom you could have good arguments, a person of substantial talent in athletics."

Royal and Fitschen spent time "around their own little campfire," TM Herbert recalls. Herbert reflects that, "Royal was a real loner. People thought it was because he saw himself as a good climber, or something, but in fact it was an aloofness that Royal had picked up when he was a kid. It didn't have anything to do with climbing. But being detached is insulting to some people."

Royal and a climber visiting from another state might walk past each other in the Yosemite campground without saying a word. Of course among the climbers who visited Yosemite were many charlatans. They were always around, people Royal and Pratt and other elite climbers had developed an ability to identify.

Fitschen offers a few impressions of "early" Royal: "He and I did a lot of things outside of climbing. We played chess, drank beer, talked a lot, and went ice skating--a rink in L.A. Royal thought ice skating would be good for his skiing. He was uncomfortable with people. A lot of the climbing community were university teachers or students. Royal wasn't a part of that community. He may have felt the pressure of that. His distance, when it did manifest itself, was a protective device."

Royal made the mistake of assuming that, just because he harbored no ill will toward others, people would be friendly toward him. His serious demeanor often was mistaken for grumpiness. He had yet to learn the lesson of life that neutrality and passiveness invited aggressiveness, as air rushes into a vacuum, and that one was better not relying upon the good will of others but rather creating good will by the positive forces of personality and action. To enjoy good will, one needed to beget it by expressing it.

Herbert adds, "Yet while he offended some, others of us followed along. Fitschen, Chouinard, Pratt, Kamps, Kor, Frost, all of us stood on Royal. He set the standards. We were looking to him. He didn't have too much to look at. As early as when he was fifteen, he was raising climbing standards--and with opposition from a few of the old Sierra Club-ers."

In August, 1960, Royal and Fitschen, along with Royal's girl friend, Janie Taylor, traveled to Grand Teton National Park in Wyoming. Fitschen recalls: "We were poor. We didn't have a camera, didn't have a car, didn't have a tent. We slept in an old, abandoned, cement kiln to stay dry when it stormed. Gary Hemming was there, a climber Royal had first met in southern California...."

Royal wrote to his mother,

"...water, clouds, mountains, and the most beautiful and varied wildflowers I have ever seen. We've been doing some fine climbing and having a grand time. We intend to stay here for about two weeks and then come to Los Angeles for a few days, after which we will go back to Yosemite to prepare for the big attempt on El Capitan. Bill Briggs, a singer and guitarist, is here, and we have terrific songfests around the campfire at night. 'Teton Tea' (a mixture of tea, sugar, lemons, and wine, quite hot) adds to the general levity...."

Royal and Joe made a first ascent on Middle Teton, the "North Face Direct." They also scaled a three hundred-foot, overhanging cliff on the left side of Garnet Canyon, called "the Big Bluff," the technical difficulty of which was matched only by a few direct-aid problems in Yosemite. During this trip, Yvon Chouinard, Fitschen, and Royal made the second ascent of the Northwest Chimney of the Grand Teton. They managed to eliminate the use of direct-aid on the route, a first free ascent considered the most difficult "alpine" climb in the park.

Royal made a number of interesting ascents in the Tetons with Janie, including the North Face of the Grand Teton and the difficult North Face of Teepe's Pillar. They also made the first ascent of the steep Northeast Face of Teepe's Pillar, in ten hours. On August 26th, Royal and Janie established a new route on the North Face of Middle Teton. A few of the features of this ten rope-length route were direct-aid overhangs and a "maximum fifth-class chimney which was overhanging and wet from snow melting above." While cold weather numbed their fingers, winds and updrafts created phenomenal cloud formations--the challenge of the elements were eased by extraordinary views. With the aid of a full moon, they made rappels, descended a seemingly interminable couloir, and arrived fatigued at their camp after midnight.

Janie was a vivacious climbing partner. At the end of September, 1960, she and Royal scaled Yosemite Point Buttress in six hours, eliminating all of the aid but on one pitch. Dave Rearick remembers that "Janie struggled and tried to be a good sport about going along on these difficult climbs, but Royal showed her no mercy." Nor did he show anyone any mercy with his terrible puns, such as "The Diehardral Route" on "Slab Happy Pinnacle." Rearick recalls an ascent of Slab Happy Pinnacle with Royal and Janie, how Royal had to pull both him and Janie a little on the rope due to the difficult moves and due to Royal's debilitating puns.

21 Royal leading on Slab Happy Pinnacle -- photo by Tom Frost

22 Royal with Janie Taylor -- photo by Harry Daley

III

By early September 1960, the incomprehensible granite of El Capitan in Yosemite had still only its 1958 ascent, by Warren Harding, Wayne Merry, and George Whitmore. Mark Powell and Bill Feuerer had participated in the early stages of that ascent, with Harding. The ascent was completed after forty-five days spread over a period of eighteen months. Six hundred and seventy-five pitons were used, and one hundred and twenty-five bolts drilled. During the ascent, the climbers would make a little upward progress, then after a few days rappel back to earth. They would leave ropes fixed on the wall and then prusik up their ropes later to establish a few new ropes higher on the wall. They would rappel again, return again, and retreat again, and go back until at last they arrived at the top of the rock. The ascent was respected by everyone, especially to know that Harding had bolted all through the night to achieve the final pitch at dawn. His perseverance was legendary. The route was a historical milestone, although the climbers had, in essence, laid siege to El Capitan.

El Capitan was so "humongous" and intimidating that even for climbers such as Robbins and Frost it was scary to think of going up there. The whole top of the wall was overhanging. In summer, the sun burned against the wall for many hours of the day.

Yet in that freight train-catching spirit of fun and adventure, Royal pictured himself and his friends climbing El Cap. All of the bolts were in place now from the first ascent, and it seemed that the next step was to do the route in a straight push without returning to the ground, without the security of fixed-ropes strung up the wall. Such an ascent would be less of an expedition and more committing. Without fixed-ropes to facilitate a retreat, they would be forced to succeed. This would require that they be self-sustained, able to carry food and water for whatever number of days the climb demanded.

The ascent would be a good confidence builder toward an eventual new and separate route on El Capitan. Royal was excited about doing the second ascent of El Cap but also was seeing beyond--to when the line his friends and he were following would be their own.

The line of the Harding route weaved a way up and across the huge wall, along the general line of El Cap's prominent, protruding, South Buttress--or "Nose." Several large pendulum swings had been required to perform traverses, to connect climbable areas of rock, or to get from the end of one crack to the beginning of another. On a continuous ascent, without fixed ropes, the completion of one of these pendulums would create a point of "no return" where, after the ropes were retrieved, there would be no easy way of getting back. To rappel would mean to try to go down hundreds of feet of blank, crackless granite. On such an attempted descent, there would be little probability of finding stances for stopping to rig rappels and no likelihood of finding piton cracks for anchoring rappels.

A few climbers in Yosemite felt that to go up on El Capitan without fixed ropes was stretching things beyond what was sensible.

Royal included Frost in his El Cap team, not forgetting the invitation he had given Tom at Tahquitz. Frost felt that he didn't have anything to worry about, because he was climbing with Royal. They also enlisted Royal's friend Joe Fitschen and that singularly gifted rock climber--Chuck Pratt.

Sixty-seven pitons and one hundred carabiners they planned to bring covered the top surface of a Camp 4 picnic-table. The leader would place pitons as he led up. He would then belay the second person up who, in turn, would hammer the pitons out. The pitons would be used over and over. Frost made some large pitons that could be used in the wide "Stove Leg" crack. Harding had climbed this crack with pitons made by Bill ("Dolt") Feuerer from the iron legs of a stove. Climbers had to employ every ingenuity.

The pitons to be used by Royal and his friends included a few small RURPS (the "realized ultimate reality piton")--about the size of a guitar pick and invented by Frost and Yvon Chouinard. Yvon had recently started a modest business manufacturing pitons and carabiners. He was immediately recognized as brilliant in his use of strong, longer-usage, chrome-moly metals and in the superior sizes and shapes of his pitons.

23 the RURP -- photo by Tom Frost

24 El Capitan, a climb of three thousand vertical feet -- photo by Tom Frost

Four duffel bags were filled with overnight gear and food, about two hundred pounds that the climbers would have to somehow transport up the wall with them--besides carrying the weight of countless pitons and carabiners. While two people climbed, two would perform the arduous task of prusiking up ropes with the bags that were stuffed with food, water, and bivouac gear. The pitons at each anchoring spot would need to be good, since they would be required to support the combined weight of four climbers and the heavy, unwieldy bags. Part of the weight was a quart and a half of water per man per day (sixty quarts), anticipating ten days on the wall.

On the lower part of the wall, they spotted football-sized rats! These predators made the climbers very wary, for they might chew on a rope at a ledge somewhere some night.

Frost thought up the strategy of prusiking with a smaller load and then rappelling and prusiking again. He was named "the human yo-yo" but at the end of that day collapsed on a ledge from fatigue. Despite the weight of so much water, it was not a lot to drink--considering the strenuousness of the proposed ascent. Robbins was, in Frost's words, "a strict disciplinarian. At bivouacs, Royal would cut off an inch of salami and pass it over to one of the climbers. He would cut off an inch of cheese and pass it over."

25 Bivouac at "Dolt Tower." L. to R.: Tom Frost, Joe Fitschen, Royal Robbins -- photo by Chuck Pratt

26 Climbers encounter El Cap troll (Chuck Pratt)
-- photo by Tom Frost

Two thousand feet above the ground, as the wall became steeper and the view straight down enough to make a stomach drop out, it was necessary to do a long double-pendulum (one pendulum to a point, followed by a second pendulum to another point). The idea of these two pendulums was to move from the top of the thin, teetering "Boot Flake" down and over to an area of rotten rock called "the Gray Bands." The first pendulum involved hanging on the rope, running as fast as possible back and forth across the wall, until the swing became so wide and its force so great as to throw the climber to the destination. The destination was a handhold that made it possible to catch at the end of the swing and clip a carabiner to another piton. The climber was now lowered from this point and ran back and forth across the wall to a small ledge. Royal later called these pendulums "the grandfather clock method of climbing."

Forced to ascend up to and around an enormous, protruding ceiling, the "Great Roof," they began the final thousand feet of vertical, overhanging rock.

27 Passing "the Great Ceiling" -- photo by Tom Frost

The four hung like mites on the most outrageous granite monolith in the world, the rock warm, friendly, its color varying from an off-white, or almost brown, to sometimes gray. The rock was exquisitely solid, as polished as marble, sculpted, according to historical geology, by an age of ice. The rock rose three thousand feet, so high that the climbers were too small to be seen from El Cap meadow in the floor of the Valley--except as specks by a discerning eye.

The four measured their progress each night by an increasingly better view of the constellation Scorpius which was visible low in the sky over the edge of a Sierra ridge to the south.

28 Beautiful rock above the Great Ceiling -- photo by Tom Frost

29 Frost with haul-bags, two thousand feet above the forest

30 Tom Frost at
"Triangular
Ledge"
(Camp 6)

31 Joe Fitschen enjoys the solitude of El Cap -- photo by Tom Frost

32 Looking down at Triangular Ledge -- photo by Tom Frost

33 Robbins -- photo by Tom Frost

The ascent was completed September 13, 1960, after six and three-quarter days instead of the anticipated ten. As with Half Dome, this ascent changed climbing. A few select spirits had passed into the next frontier. They had opened a door to an era of more committing ascents of big walls.

It was the most striking climb on the face of the earth, as far as Royal and his friends could ascertain, yet the media knew nothing of the ascent. There was some degree of satisfaction in this for the climbers, that they had escaped the eye of the masses. A measure of obscurity was necessary, they felt, to honor what was "sacred." Yet they were not alone, greeted at the top by a group of over twenty friends--including Harding, Chouinard, and Janie Taylor. They had hiked the eight-mile trail up the backside. Later in the newsletter *Mugelnoos*, Royal wrote: "Besides congratulations, the climbers were given champagne, beer, milk, fruit juices, nectarines, and cantaloupes, twenty-five pounds of ice keeping the drinks well chilled."

34 The rewards of success, Joe Fitschen, Royal Robbins, Chuck Pratt, Tom Frost, summit of El Cap

In Yosemite, Royal's adventurous spirit had come to a land full of possibilities, dreams, and private, first reactions. His eyes and desires charted the new country, the vertical, critical Yosemite lines that would become symbols of a remarkable youth and that he and a few friends would enjoy for a few years exclusively. It was as though Royal and Pratt and Frost and their friends had built Yosemite out of their imaginations and then contentedly started to live in it. Those white, pink, cloudy, sometimes seemingly endless, fairy tale surfaces of granite, upon which their lives had hit perhaps intuitively, would be cause for them to return again and again, rock climbs that in the late '50s and early '60s accommodated their most personal hopes while at the same time establishing a model for the rest of the world of climbers. There were many other good climbers in other parts of the country and outside the country, and other groups of talented individuals in Yosemite itself. But the victories of Royal and these few friends were singular. They were achievements that would come to interpret the direction in which American and world rock climbing were to go.

IV

An important part of the path of Royal Robbins was the way it unfolded in the outdoors, a relationship with nature as well as to people or to the testing of skills. The vivid, arresting views of Yosemite, the thick, deep green flora, a coyote, a deer, the wide, varied light transported in the clouds, always were there to enlarge and enrich the experience of climbing. It was to the advantage of the person who was aware of and who gave veneration to these phenomena: a rattlesnake sliding away in the talus at the foot of El Cap, pools of the Merced River reflecting blue oak trees and reflecting the granite walls, water almost blooming with these images, soft air blowing, the smell of vanilla from a Jeffrey pine, the smell of rock when it was hit by a hammer, the great Yosemite waterfalls bursting with a sudden, more noticeable roar, in spring sunlight the spray of a waterfall lifted sideways by wind to form a veil of white moving serenely across the sky. It was a transaction between place and spirit as much as the attainment of goals in climbing.

Emerson: "Who looks upon a river in a meditative hour and is not reminded of the flux of all things? Throw a stone into the stream, and the circles that propagate themselves are the beautiful type of all influence."

35 Clouds beginning to lift off of Sentinel Rock -- photo by Pat Ament

One fascination for Royal was to watch a storm develop, enormous cumulus heralding thunder, preceded always by a south wind, the grasses of a meadow blowing, trees swaying back and forth, and a jagged line of lightning imprinted with sudden grace in the darkness at the center of a cloud.

To this point, Royal could have retired and been viewed as preeminent--a legend--in climbing. But once one starts to imagine, there continue to flow ideas. Life, inevitably, is made in their image.

He often congregated with his friends "and others" in Camp 4--the Yosemite campground they adopted as their own and from where they planned climbs and pondered the incredible opportunities that rose in the form of granite all around. A few of these people were beginning to be viewed as nothing short of "luminaries": the private, brilliant Chuck Pratt, the wry, goodhearted Tom Frost. In the October 1960 *Mugelnoos*, Royal wrote of Fitschen: "Joe Fitschen will be working for Curry Company in Yosemite Valley this winter. He is presently a busboy in the Yosemite Lodge coffee shop but hopes to work his way up to bellboy at the Ahwahnee Hotel, all this to pay for a trip to Europe next summer...."

The ten to twenty-foot tall boulders around the campground had enticing climbing problems and attracted playful competition. Royal and whoever was bouldering with him would attempt a problem using only one hand, the other hand held behind the back. Royal devised a route (and showed-up a few companions) by hopping from hold to hold with only a single foot (and no hands).

As with Tahquitz Rock, the smooth, glacier-polished granite of Yosemite required--and somewhat forced--the refinement of a climber's technique. The "lieback," for example, with feet pushing horizontally into the wall and hands pulling in opposition outward against a hold or crack, required exact body position and had to be learned by either falling off totally or by discovering the kind of perfection that worked. On "the boulders," Royal added to his repertoire of footwork and other skills. On "mantel" problems, with the heels of his hands on a small slope of rock, shoulder flexibility allowed him to rotate his wrists so that his fingers pointed inward to his stomach and his elbows came together in front of his face. According to Royal, "My ability to mantel and also to perform the 'arm-lock,' which I invented, helped me to keep up with Pratt."

An attraction more compelling than granite had begun to reveal itself along the periphery of Royal's Yosemite visits. She was a University of California student by the name of Liz Burkner, who was working a summer job as hostess at the Ahwahnee Hotel in Yosemite. Liz hiked when she had free time, and bicycled, and explored the Valley floor. A self-described "small-town girl" and only child, her mother had spoon-fed her the San Francisco cultural life of ballet, music, opera, galleries, luxurious clothes, hotels, restaurants, and international travel. Suddenly she found herself in the camaraderie of a group of scruffy rock climbers.

Liz remained by day the well-dressed, social hostess at the Ahwahnee, the poised sophisticate, while in the evenings drawn to the big, round, granite boulders of Camp 4 where the rock climbers congregated. She found herself eager to learn more about these inner-directed, ostensibly unaffected men who had a mysterious connection with the mountains and who transmitted a sense of strength. She began to date a climber by the name of Herb Swedlund.

After work one night, she walked through the forest to where the climbers were gathered around a campfire. Royal was sitting with his girlfriend, Janie Taylor, but was unable to take his eyes off Liz. She was, to him, very beautiful. His gaze was unsettling to Liz, especially since he was sitting with another woman, yet the magnetism between Royal and Liz was undeniable for both of them.

He had immense respect and love for Janie, although they had agreed that they were friends first--with no implied vows.

Royal soon began to seek Liz's company. She was reluctant, yet finally consented to spend time with him. She found his elemental honesty humorous and was attracted to his forwardness, his saying such things as "I want you" (with his foot on the bumper of the Mercedes her father was letting her use).

June 6th and 7th of '61, Royal and Tom Frost ascended the steep Northwest Wall of Yosemite's very slender, towering Higher Cathedral Spire. Royal wrote in *Summit Magazine* that the climb was "roughly the peer of the Northwest Face of Half Dome." Its dark-colored granite, lack of sun, and distinct challenges gave the route a forbidding mystique. And it pressed the climbers to their limits. The mystique grew in the imagination of other climbers who heard or read in *Summit Magazine* about the "white overhangs" and the dangerous, unprotected, overhanging "Chimney of Horrors." This latter feature was flaring and rounded, not deep, and the rock on the inside of the chimney at the start was granular. The chimney leaned upward to the right, with overhangs below it, the climber feeling that space opened up below and that the chimney had no bottom. Frost recalls, "It (the Chimney of Horrors) made you real nervous. The leader had no protection, except one bolt, for maybe a hundred feet. And then if the second climber fell, he would swing a long way out into space and be hanging over the bottomless void. The chimney was, for me, well-named."

On two initial attempts of the route, first with Fitschen and then with Frost, difficulties of one sort or another forced retreat. Part way up the wall, for example, they discovered that they had left behind the bigger pitons. And then on the next attempt, they accidentally left behind the bolts.

On the successful ascent, neither Royal nor Frost wanted to climb the Chimney of Horrors again. But it was necessary, and according to Frost, "Royal was so indomitable that he would do what he had to do." One aid-pitch took five hours to complete. On that pitch, eight knife-blade pitons were used and six of the tiny, super knife-blade RURPS. Royal wrote that the situation of being on that climb "was psychologically devastating," although Frost also noted later that "Royal didn't lend the appearance of that."

36 Robbins leading on Higher Cathedral Spire -- photo by Tom Frost

37 Frost uneasy, through the White Overhangs -- photo by Royal Robbins

56

38 Royal Robbins -- photo by Tom Frost

     June 24th, 1961, Royal and Chuck Wilts made the first ascent of the North Ridge of Half Dome (the upper lefthand skyline, as seen from the floor of Yosemite Valley). On the same day, Bob Kamps and Dave Rearick did the first ascent of the West Corner of Half Dome. Royal and Chuck arrived at the top before the other team and walked down slabs to the west to greet Kamps and Rearick as they approached. The four began their descent together, toward the cable route on the east side of the rock, when Royal had the notion that he would attempt to walk down the east slabs without touching his hands. This was no easy thing to do, a feat that would demand supreme footwork, balance, and courage. Rearick describes the event:

"I witnessed it. My heart was in my throat. He was wearing Austrian 'Zillertal' climbing shoes and was carrying a rope and a pack. His fall line at certain points would have taken him off the South Wall. There was no sitting or skidding along on his rump. I felt very nervous watching him. The rock that the earliest climbers had once thought unconquerable was being walked down. That was all Robbins. He had the confidence."

In late summer of 1961, Royal invited Liz to climb a moderate route above Yosemite in the high country peaks of Tuolumne. Liz was not fit and got "frighteningly winded" walking up, although she tried not to reveal her plight to Royal. When she reached the top of Cathedral Peak, she felt as though she had conquered a major mountain. Little did she suspect at this time that she would become the first woman to climb a Grade VI: the colossal, sheer, two thousand-foot high, Northwest Face of Half Dome.

In September of '61, Steve Roper and Frank Sacherer made an outlandish, eight-hour ascent of the seventeen hundred-foot Salathe-Steck route on the North Face of Sentinel. TM Herbert remembers: "Royal was a little bothered that Roper was talking about that Sentinel ascent. You know how dramatic Roper can be. He was always trying to get your goat." Royal was, on the one hand, stunned by the accomplishment and, on the other hand, eager to surpass it. He brought Roper and Sacherer a bottle of champagne, as a way of expressing his respect, and then two days later, with Tom Frost, made his own speed ascent in the astonishing time of three hours and fourteen minutes. Royal and Frost climbed simultaneously up many of the pitches, roped together and clipping the rope through occasional gear, but without belaying, almost a double-solo but for the crux sections where they did belay. In Frost's words, "Royal wanted to do it in five hours, but I said--impossible."

As though bringing Tom along had made it easier, Royal later did the route again alone. He belayed himself only on three sections, the "Wilson Overhang," the direct-aid headwall, and near the top at a last difficult crack.

According to Herbert: "Royal was really the only one in the '50s and early '60s in Yosemite and at Tahquitz who did any free rock-soloing."

Robbins, Pratt, and Frost were focusing on a possible new route up the three thousand-foot Southwest Face of El Cap, or "the Salathe Wall," as Royal and Chouinard began to call it. The name was a tribute to John Salathe, pioneer of the first ascent of the North Face of Sentinel Rock with Al Steck. Salathe was also known for his first ascent of the Lost Arrow Chimney and was recognized as not only an innovator but a kind of "father" of Yosemite rock climbing.

39 Pioneer John Salathe with innovator Yvon Chouinard in Camp 4 -- photo by Tom Frost

Royal was determined to make this new route on El Capitan a true adventure and not a bolted expedition. Given enough bolts and time, any rock of any size or difficulty could be climbed. To have the certitude of bolts, and to string fixed ropes from the bottom of the wall to its top, diminished the adventure, he felt. A greater joy would exist in a single, continuous push--with the fewest bolts possible. Such notions seemed in keeping with the great European and English climbers, such as Buhl and Bonatti and Young and Mummery, who had made a tradition of boldness and who felt that technology--if there was too much of it--did not give a mountain, or a rock, a fighting chance.

Yet it remained of real concern how they would get down if--somewhere high on the route--they were forced to retreat. The extended, traversing nature of the middle section of the proposed climb would lead them above a thousand feet of barren, crackless rock. A descent down that appeared to be absurd. Pendulums and points of "no return," as well as increasingly overhanging rock, made the route a serious commitment, more so than the Nose route. Rescue by others was not considered to be a viable option, if even a possible one. How would such a tremendous deed as a rescue be effected? And by whom? The climbers would have to take care of themselves.

Royal, Pratt, and Frost felt that they made a good ensemble for the route.

40 Camp 4, Chuck Pratt and Royal Robbins prepare for the Salathe Wall -- photo by Tom Frost

41 The Salathe Wall of El Capitan -- photo by Tom Frost

It was decided, mostly by Royal, that an acceptable plan would be to do the route in two stages, going up the first nine hundred feet of climbing, trying to establish a number of rappels down the blank wall, and then returning to the climb for a final push. This would involve bringing extra ropes to ensure that a rappel could be made. On the 12th of September, they began.

42 Robbins traverses on the third pitch of the Salathe -- photo by Tom Frost

43 Robbins on the Salathe -- photo by Tom Frost

The first nine hundred feet of the route were characterized by a lot of high-quality rock with beautiful, unexpected angles and one section that essentially had no holds. This "slab pitch" required using only shoe adhesion ("friction") to ascend.

4 Robbins ventures up onto a virgin El Cap, "the friction pitch," thousands of feet of ock overhead -- photo by Tom Frost

45 Robbins route-finding -- photo by Tom Frost

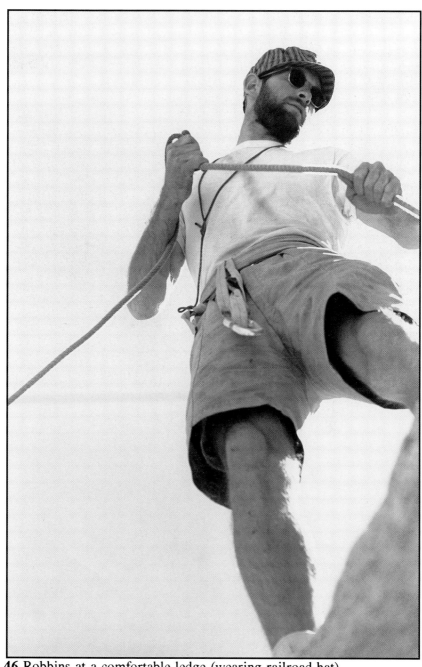

46 Robbins at a comfortable ledge (wearing railroad hat)
-- photo by Tom Frost

Several days later, an angling rappel and some leftward traversing brought them to "Lung Ledge." According to their intentions, they began to try to establish a rappel route down a smooth wall. There was nothing much in the way of a ledge, but a few cracks for pitons could be found. A few bolts had to be placed. They fixed a single rope down each rappel and left each rope in place.

47 Robbins -- photo by Tom Frost

They returned a few days later to the route on the 19th of September, prusiked up the ropes to the high point, retrieved the ropes as they prusiked, and tossed the extra ropes off the wall to be fetched later. The climb was now all or nothing, upward into unknown realms of rock.

48 Upward into unknown realms of rock

The clean, white rock of El Captian was conducive to their philosophy of joy and purity of ideal. The air was clear and wholesome. A fresh, almost oceany breeze rushed softly below through the leaves of oak trees. Blue of the sky spread out immaculately above. Swallows were companions to the climbers on the wall, swirling past them, diving into cracks, making resentful noises from within the cracks as a piton was hammered. The size and grandeur and waterfalls of Yosemite, its abundance of wildlife and fernlife and mystery and forests, in combination with the adventure of El Capitan, were the experience.

49 Robbins pendulums into Hollow Flake Crack
-- photo by Tom Frost

Midway up the wall, they confronted a frightening formation called "the Ear"--a huge flake whose bottom flared open from the main wall. To climb past this obstacle meant to go in behind the flake, wedge the body, and squirm upward, or "chimney," thirty feet right, with the view below consisting of a couple of thousand feet of unnerving space.

50 Inside the terrifying "Ear"

51 Behind El Cap Spire

52 El Cap Spire, Pratt and Robbins studying the upper wall for a route -- photo by Tom Frost

53 Pratt leading above El Cap Spire -- photo by Tom Frost

72

54 Looking down at El Cap Spire, Robbins resting
-- photo by Tom Frost

55 Overhangs everywhere

56 Tom Frost, ledge with sun, El Capitan -- photo by Royal Robbins

57 Robbins pendulums, high on El Cap -- photo by Tom Frost

58 Robbins belays, hanging from pitons, below the roof at the start of the overhanging headwall -- photo by Tom Frost

59 Tom Frost moves right, below roof -- photo by Royal Robbins

60 Haul-line hangs vertically off overhanging Headwall

Above the roof was "the Headwall"--two hundred feet of overhanging rock. From the tremendously exhilarating position of exposure in the middle of the Headwall, twenty-five hundred feet above the ground, the huge Sierra trees, which stood in a straight drop far below, were like blades of grass.

61 Robbins in wind on the Headwall, forest far below
-- photo by Tom Frost

62 Chuck Pratt nears the end of three thousand feet of climbing --
photo by Tom Frost

On September 24, 1961, after six days of climbing, they completed the Salathe Wall. In thirty-four roped leads, they had used four hundred and eighty-four pitons but remarkably only thirteen bolts (compared to Harding's hundred and twenty-five). The route had woven an elegant, majestic, thrilling new line up the immense wall of El Capitan. Yet they recognized that the climb was not a "continuous" ascent in the purest sense, due to their use of fixed ropes on the first third of the route. Royal felt that it was necessary to improve on the style. He was always in the forefront of philosophical thinking, and in Pratt and Frost had ready converts.

63 Heads crowned with flower-wreaths from friends, the climbers toss champagne glasses over the edge
-- photo by Dorene Frost

About mid-December of '61, Royal moved to Sugar Bowl ski resort atop California's Donner Pass, near Norden, where he tended bar and instructed skiing.

Liz had returned to school in Berkeley. It was a restless, uneasy period for her, having left the mountains and Royal behind. Her studies seemed to lack purpose. She was at cross-purposes with herself, considering that Royal was with someone else. She couldn't believe how much she missed him. It was alarming for her to realize that she was not in control, that she was in love.

In January and February of '62, Janie spent time at Sugar Bowl. Royal found her a job baby-sitting for his boss, and she also worked in the dining room. She then left for Europe with her father, with the aim that Royal would later meet her in Europe after the ski season or sometime in summer.

Royal wrote Liz and invited her to Sugar Bowl for a weekend. She went, and it became clear that they were destined to be more than friends.

Liz returned to school. Royal missed her and asked her to come back and ski with him for the rest of the winter. She wanted to learn to ski. Three months prior to graduation, Liz packed her bags and left school for good. A college degree seemed unimportant. School had never been for her an end in itself. She had no particular focus of study, and leaving was, as she viewed it, the next big step forward in her life.

The skiing was magnificent, and Liz felt a change in herself--that she had begun to "live for the moment," to "seize the day."

Royal's heart was with Liz. But also he had thoughts about Janie, knowing that she might be hurt. He respected Janie and wanted to preserve her unique individual dignity. Royal and Janie had long been arranging a trip to Europe, where they would climb and meet Fitschen (who had gone to Spain already to live for a time). Royal told Liz that when summer came he was going to keep that plan. He wanted to go to Europe, and he wanted time with Janie so that if their relationship was over it would be between the two of them.

For the most part, Royal was honest with Janie, as was he with Liz, in regard to his feelings. There was no deception. It wasn't his way, in climbing or in love.

Between May 5th and 7th, 1962, with Tom Frost, Royal succeeded at a new climb on the North Wall of Sentinel. During their three days on the wall, the only mishap was at a severe overhang where the weight of Royal's body pulled a piton. He fell twenty-five feet, tearing out a couple of other pitons, before Frost was able to stop the fall with the rope.

64 Robbins leading on a new route on Sentinel -- photo by Tom Frost

65 The overhang where Royal fell -- photo by Tom Frost

66 Robbins on the
"12-inch Ledge"
(Sentinel)
-- photo by Tom Frost

They called the fourteen-pitch route the "North Wall, Direct," although it later became known as the "Mozart Wall"--a name adopted by Eric Beck, Jim Bridwell, and other climbers to mock Royal's love of classical music.

67 Royal Robbins, summit of Sentinel (El Capitan in background)
-- photo by Tom Frost

V

Royal departed for Europe in May '62, first hitchhiking from California to New York. Along the way, in the desert of southeast Utah, he and Jack Turner made the first ascent of "Mexican Hat"--a red slab of rock sitting flat on a pedestal of rock and presenting a huge overhang on all sides.

When Royal reached the East Coast, he wrote to his mother: "Last night we had an incredible thunderstorm, and I was amazed at how the thunder rolls and rolls and rolls before stopping. Manhattan Island is a fascinating place where the pace is very fast (everyone is on the make) and money and power are fearfully evident...." Continuing by sea voyage, on a Yugoslav freighter bound for Tangier, he was not attracted to the company of the other passengers on the ship. One can imagine him standing alone near the bow of the ship and gazing quietly out across the ocean. In a postcard to his mother, he noted that he saw "many flying fish." At night, seeing the flashes of light emanating as the prow of the ship sliced the water, he thought of the line "the phosphorus flashed in her seaweed hair," from the song "the Keeper of the Eddystone Light."

The plan was to meet Fitschen and Janie in Tangier. Through a misunderstanding, they were not there. Royal took a train and caught up with them in Madrid. But Fitschen now had met a woman on the island of Ibiza, near the north coast of Spain, and no longer wanted to go to the Alps. He wanted rather to spend the summer at Ibiza. Royal was unhappy with Fitschen and also had lost the convenience of Fitschen's car.

He hitchhiked with Janie up through Spain. After six days, they arrived in Paris where they enjoyed the role of sightseers. Royal wrote to his mother of the cathedral of Notre Dame and of his appreciation of the opportunity of seeing Van Gogh, Monet, and Renoir originals. Royal and Janie took a train to Chamonix where it was raining a lot. Tired of the rain, they went by train to the southern coast of France, on the Mediterranean near Marseilles, where they found white limestone cliffs rising out of "beautifully clear and amazingly calm water." As Royal wrote to his mother, they had "a lovely time climbing and swimming."

Soon Royal ran into Gary Hemming, his acquaintance from the Tetons. Hemming was a dynamic individual, and Royal was swept up in his energy and drive.

68 Gary Hemming, Chamonix -- photo by
Ken Wilson

Hemming was living in Europe now, and, in late July 1962, he and
Royal attempted a new route on the Petit Dru. After spending one night on the
mountain, a violent storm chased them back down. Camped beneath the Dru,
they witnessed the most terrific lightning storm Royal had ever seen.

On an occasion of better weather, they were at the ascent again. Between
the North and West Faces, the route followed steep rock for seventeen hundred
feet and met the West Face route at a distinctive landmark called the 90-Meter
Dihedral. Joining parts of five different routes, the climbing totalled three
thousand feet. Royal estimated the two-and-a-half day climb to be as strenuous
as the Northwest Face of Half Dome. In the December 1962 *Sierra Club
Bulletin*, he said that it was the "finest" route he had made "under alpine
conditions."

59 The Dru -- courtesy of Diadem archives

90

70 Hemming leading on the Dru -- photo by Royal Robbins

71 Bivouac on the Dru, Robbins enjoys something hot out of a bent pot -- photo by Gary Hemming

72 Robbins leading on the Dru -- photo by Gary Hemming

During a dramatic rescue of some lads in bad weather, Hemming and a couple of companions followed the initial part of this route and, by so doing, creatively expedited the rescue. Hemming's knowledge of the route enabled him and his partners to climb fast and avoid the Dru's dreaded "death couloir." The rescue brought immediate renown to Hemming in Europe.

While in Europe, Royal thought about Liz. It was difficult for him to write to her, because Janie was always around. He was sorry that he was going to be losing Janie as a companion. Yet Janie knew about Royal's feeling for Liz, and there needed to be no major rupture. It was not necessary that one friendship totally eclipse another, although pain would exist. At last he wrote and told Liz that he had made up his mind: "The longer I'm away, the more I realize what you mean to me…. I've told Janie, and we will be returning home shortly. She has asked that she and I do one last climb together in the Valley before you arrive. After that, she is leaving."

Liz and Royal met in Yosemite. The more they were together, the more they developed a relationship that they saw could be lasting. They were comfortable together. Liz admired his lack of facade, his intensity, as well as sensitivity, a "care for others." He seemed to her comfortable with himself. And while complex, he was sure of his life's direction. Royal saw "the woman of his dreams," that they were "soul-mates." It was attractive to him that she could live with his interests and relate to his strong, "controlling passion" for climbing. He saw that she had a sense of adventure.

73 Liz Burkner

Doing the Salathe Wall of El Capitan in a true, continuous ascent was still on Royal's mind. It bothered him that he, Pratt, and Frost had used those fixed lines on the lower portion of the wall.

74 Camp 4, Robbins and TM Herbert plan for a continuous ascent of the Salathe -- photo by Tom Frost

In September of '62, with Pratt in the army, TM Herbert, Frost, and Royal began an ascent of the Salathe but suffered unseasonable heat. Whenever a cloud came over that looked as though it might hold rain, they opened their mouths and stuck out their tongues--hoping to catch any drops that fell. Royal contracted a vague, immobilizing illness, possibly from laughing too hard at the commentaries--the side-splitting, ongoing genius--of Herbert.

75 TM Herbert leading on lower wall of the Salathe
-- photo by Tom Frost

76 Robbins considers a move
-- photo by Tom Frost

77 A sick Robbins continues
onward -- photo by Tom Frost

Then at a bivouac on "Hollow Flake Ledge" about fourteen hundred feet up the wall, the heat turned to hail. Violent, prolonged downpours continued all night with bright electrical displays and thunder that reverberated up and down the Valley. They spent most of the next day sleeping and trying to recuperate, but TM also became ill.

78 Robbins at Hollow Flake Ledge -- photo by Tom Frost

79 Sick, and no way out, TM hangs himself -- photo by Tom Frost

A descent of many hours of cautious, methodical rappel work, including a large, delicate rappel-pendulum to Lung Ledge, ended their attempt.

Royal's resolution was in no way dampened. He was on the Salathe a month later, on October 9th, with Frost. Clouds covered the sky each day and threatened a storm, but the route led the climbers upward into glorious places.

80 El Capitan -- photo by Tom Frost

After two thousand feet of climbing, high on the wall at dark, and coming to a complicated section of the route that involved a pendulum, they decided to push onward rather than attempt a hanging bivouac. The weather was threatening, and they hoped to reach "Sous Le Toit Ledge." Frost sat on a small place, as Royal found his way up through the granite enigma. Salvation came in the ɔrm of a full moon that gave them light through the clouds.

The threatening weather made things more uncertain, but also more exciting. The next day, they moved up onto "the Headwall"-- one of the most remarkable places ever attained by climbers. Overhanging slightly, it was the feature that stuck in their minds all the way up the wall. From the middle of the Headwall, it was almost three thousand feet straight below to the trees. A climber had to be in good form to completely enjoy it.

Above, at the last bivouac, unusually ferocious weather struck. Royal later wrote in the *American Alpine Journal* that the storm was "...bent on tearing us from the ledge." Rain fell steadily, and there was snow in the morning. Then in a burst of revelation, the weather cleared and became the most perfect they had experienced in the Sierra. On the 13th of October, 1962, four and a half days after they had begun, they stood atop El Capitan together for the third time.

El Capitan exemplified life's extremes of tribulation, as well as joy. As to the latter, Royal wrote: "The air was cool, but the direct sunlight was warm and friendly. All the high country was white with new snow, and two or three inches had fallen along the rim of the Valley, on Half Dome, and on Cloud's Rest. One could see for great distances, and each peak was sharply etched against a dark-blue sky. We were feeling spiritually very rich indeed as we hiked down through the grand Sierra forests to the Valley."

81 Half Dome and High Sierra with new snow -- photo by Harry Daley

To feel "spiritually very rich" presented an interesting contradiction to those who knew Royal to be a professed agnostic. Often the word "spiritual" was connected to the idea of God, or belief. One might speculate that climbing was building in Royal, slowly, the foundations of a true spiritual outlook--something that he would indeed embrace later. He needed words to match deep feelings, yet the uses of "spiritual" in his writings were also foreshadowings. From the first, Royal's closer friends were drawn to him because of his strength and because of qualities that had a feeling of morality or of spiritual integrity. He cared about truth. It was as beautiful to him and as vital as the aesthetic beauty he perceived in nature. Yet for these qualities to include actual belief would require a progression of years.

Climbing was, for many people, something in which to dabble--a romantic dilettantism. For Royal, it was a way of life--a consciousness closely related to the religious impulse. Although agnostic, his discipline was toward mental, technical, and "spiritual" virtuosity. He was deviled with resistance against less competent climbers who were trying to bolt the spirit out of the game. He found any hint of dishonesty deplorable. His searching, as he wrote in an article, was for "the highest human expression." In Yosemite, indeed there was a spiritualization of adventure.

The ecstatic condition had, for Royal, its divine name: climbing.

After the Salathe, Robbins and Frost did the second ascent (and first continuous ascent) of another Warren Harding route: the intimidating, often overhanging East Face of Washington Column. Harding watched from below as Robbins and Frost climbed past many of his bolts and removed them. Royal was beginning to take action and to make a statement about the overuse of the drill.

82 Robbins leads on the East Face of Washington Column -- photo by Tom Frost

83 Robbins takes notes, on the East Face of Washington Column
-- photo by Tom Frost

The Sierra Nevada "prophet" John Muir wrote that "in the face of Yosemite scenery cautious remonstrance is vain." And so was Royal drawn into, and upward onto, Yosemite's realms. In May of '63, he made a stunning solo ascent of the preposterously overhanging Leaning Tower in Yosemite.

Harding, Glen Denny, and Al MacDonald had spent eighteen days over a period of ten months to siege the first ascent of the route, employing fixed ropes and many bolts. Royal soloed the route, its second ascent, an incredible commitment to the unknown that he managed in three and a half days through horrendous weather that obliterated the rock and the wall. He was feeling more confident than ever and referred to the ascent as an inspiration for him.

He remembers, "Perhaps more than any other climb, I was at the top of my form." He knew he was ready to do something that would take him far out on a limb. He felt good, no apprehension, no anxiety, even though it was one of the most committing things he had ever attempted. The severely overhung nature of the wall made a retreat practically impossible, as a rappel rope would hang out in space away from the rock.

No one knew that he was on the wall except Liz, and he preferred it that way. It added to the sense of aloneness. She felt he was safe, because she trusted his mastery. Even as the storm grew worse, she had faith in his ability to carry out his scheme. He spent nights sitting--hanging--in a "belay seat" (a miniature hammock).

An afternoon during the climb, Royal fell asleep in his slings and had a dream where he was trying to walk on a floor that kept stretching and collapsing under him. He woke to find himself thrashing about in his slings.

When he finished the climb, he was nearly swept a thousand feet off Bridalveil Falls. As he attempted to cross Bridalveil Creek, the quickest line of descent from the summit of the Leaning Tower, the river was running high. He doubled his 7mm haul-rope high around a tree to use as a hand line. Half way across the river, he realized how serious the situation was. If he were to lose his footing, the rope would tighten and cause him to be held under the rapidly moving water. If he let go of the rope, he would be washed over the falls. There was no room for error. He had to keep moving and remain calm. As the force of the water against his legs became stronger, he discovered the stratagem of raising one of his legs. Each time he took a step, he quickly lifted his back leg from the swift, powerful current. This gave him a stronger stance against the force of the river. Another climber several years later, attempting this same crossing, drowned and ended up hanging from his rope just below the crest of the falls.

Royal's ascent of the Leaning Tower was the first solo of a major Yosemite wall and one of the most important achievements ever in climbing. Walking down the road, after the ascent, he ran into Colorado climber Layton

Kor just west of Camp 4. Noticing Royal's pack and ropes, Layton could see that Royal had been climbing for several days. There was only one wall a person could climb, and find some partial protection, in the weather that they had been having. Layton immediately guessed that Royal was returning from the Leaning Tower.

84 Yosemite's Leaning Tower -- photo by Tom Frost

104

85 Royal Robbins, the great days in Yosemite -- photo by Tom Frost

During this period, Royal found time for an ascent of the two thousand-foot Direct North Buttress of Middle Cathedral Rock with Kor.

86 The North Buttress of Middle Cathedral -- photo by Pat Ament

Among countless miscellaneous climbs or smaller first ascents, Royal created a June 1963 new route up Yosemite's Far West Face of Rixon's Pinnacle with tall, thin, very competent Richard (Dick) McCracken. The route was noted for its exciting finish: a difficult, vigorous pendulum to where it was possible to grab a thin flake, climb to the top of the flake, then hand-traverse ten feet right to the summit.

McCracken was to become an important figure in Royal's climbing and joined Royal for a new idea: a two thousand-foot line on the open expanse of unclimbed wall to the right of the Northwest Face route on Half Dome. This would be the "Direct" Northwest Face. Two other climbers--Ed Cooper, from Washington, and Californian Galen Rowell--had begun fixing ropes on this very route. As Royal felt, they were attempting to bring back the expeditionary themes that climbers had wished to transcend.

87 Half Dome with clouds -- photo by Pat Ament

June 11th, 1963, when Cooper and Rowell were taking a break from their efforts, Royal and McCracken rather impolitely stepped in and began their own attempt of the route. They did not care how Cooper or Rowell might respond.

88 Direct North Face of Half Dome, Robbins leading beside Cooper's fixed ropes -- photo by Richard McCracken

Royal had begun to devise new, even more imaginative methods of climbing over blank rock. One such method was to carefully place a small fifi-hook on a minute crystal (or flake or ledge) and stand in a sling attached to the hook. The prayer was that the hook wouldn't pop off. Royal had mastered the use of the Chouinard-Frost RURP--that tiny piton the size of a guitar pick--and had developed his skill at finding small knobs to gingerly set slings around. These were resources that made direct-aid an art and that greatly lessened the need for bolts.

Royal exhibited a very rational sense in an endeavor thought to be obscure and irrational by society at large. He was applying a scale of values, almost a metaphysic, whereby climbing might be the exercising ground of rigorous thought.

89 Royal maneuvering on Half Dome -- photo by Richard McCracken

The intensity of his techniques were expressed on this new route on Half Dome. One section of rock involved bad pitons, a pendulum, delicate free-climbing, and a fifi-hook used just the right way on a microscopic nubbin in order to ascend without bolts. Higher on the route, shaky pitons led to a great white flake--thin, hollow, and mostly detached. A treacherous place to piton, he used fifi-hooks and slings to traverse twenty feet along the top of the flake. A couple of pitons "found unstable residence" behind shaky flakes, and then "a bolt provided security for six RURPS and a knifeblade that followed."

90 Richard McCracken leading on Half Dome
-- photo by Royal Robbins

91 McCracken follows "traverse of no return" (the climbers felt committed, since a rappel straight down meant crossing much crackless, blank rock) -- photo by Royal Robbins

Meanwhile, Liz was having her own adventure. She and Frank Sacherer had hiked the eight mile trail and then scrambled up the cable route on the east side of Half Dome with the hope of being able to peer down from the summit and observe the last pitches of the climb. Suddenly a storm blew in with unexpected force. Aware of the dangers of lightning on a summit, she and Frank advised a number of hiker-sightseers to get down as fast as possible. Everyone began running down the cables. Just as Frank got down and Liz let go of the cable at the bottom, lightning hit--tossing the hikers above her like leaves in the wind. Although badly burned and unconscious, the hikers all miraculously survived.

Royal and McCracken reached the top a few hours later, after four days on the wall.

92 Richard McCracken near the top of Half Dome -- photo by Royal Robbins

One of the rewards of this ascent for Royal and McCracken was that they had made the route an adventure. They felt that they had saved the route from a fixed-rope--and possibly bolted--siege. The only thing perhaps that tainted the ascent was their treatment of Cooper and Rowell. Cooper was a bit discouraged and left Yosemite. Both Cooper and Rowell were reasonably good climbers, but whose styles were a bit behind the times. They would continue to climb and be successful in the commercial pursuit of photography.

VI

One evening in the lounge of Yosemite Lodge, a Curry Company employee announced to Royal and some friends that there had been a radio report of an attempt which was to be made on the right side of the Upper Yosemite Falls. This attempt, the report said, was going to be made by Ed Cooper, Glen Denny, and Jim Baldwin. Hearing this, Denny (who did not like publicity) and Baldwin dropped out. Cooper later fixed ropes two pitches up the wall with Eric Bjornstad, but threatening weather ended the effort, and Cooper later removed his fixed ropes. For Royal and McCracken, a rest was in order after the extraordinary achievement of a new, difficult route in continuous style up the direct face of Half Dome. But instead of repose, they started up the large, unclimbed wall of Upper Yosemite Falls.

On June 21st, 1963, the first day of climbing for Robbins and McCracken, the falls were crashing thunderously "in all their springtime glory." It was a spectacular, exhilarating, very different kind of place to be, directly beside the falls, receiving some of the spray. As Royal led up the first pitch, wind began to blow from the west. Water from the falls showered McCracken who was belaying at the start of the climb. The freezing water rained onto him for twenty frigid minutes, completely drenching him and filling his shoes with ice water. He shivered violently. McCracken was a fast climber and used his speed, racing up the wall, to try to thaw out. Royal later wrote that McCracken's "riant" eyes were still sparkling. McCracken had to look the word up.

93 Upper Yosemite Falls -- photo by Tom Frost

94 Robbins leading around overhangs, Upper Yosemite Falls
-- photo by Richard McCracken

95 Robbins on sloping bivouac ledge (they had to try not to roll off), Upper Yosemite Falls -- photo by Richard McCracken

96 Sir Royal seiges fortress (Upper Yosemite Falls)
-- photo by Richard McCracken

The climbing was almost secondary to the loud, wet, dynamic atmosphere. The route ended with five hours of aid-traversing west to a point just above the crest of the falls where Yosemite Creek, rushing along, "suddenly found itself in mid-air." It was noon the 23rd of June.

In a later article for the *American Alpine Journal*, Royal offered a few thoughts from this climb: "Some 2500 feet below was another world.... Automobiles crept along the wet asphalt like ants. Somber and impassive, the granite walls stood as they have for millions of years, seemingly eternal, while Nature's creatures passed part of their momentary and insignificant existence between them."

He added that the adventure of the climb awakened their minds and "spirits" to "a lust for life and a keener awareness of beauty."

Royal hadn't yet been to Colorado and in July of '63 decided to start there as the beginning of a tour through several climbing areas outside his beloved Yosemite. He and Liz set off on this adventure together, hitchhiking to Colorado, catching rides with insane drivers, and sleeping in ditches.

Royal immediately teamed with Layton Kor to attempt the one thousand-foot, sheer Diamond wall on the East Face of Longs Peak.

97 East Face of Longs Peak, Colorado -- photo by Edd Hamilton

Layton phoned me and asked if I would serve on their "support party." The Rocky Mountain Park rangers required that the climbers have a support party. I was to meet Layton and Royal near Chasm Lake, at the tiny, stone shelter-cabin five miles up the mountain.

I walked the trail, alone, upward, into the cool air of the mountain, through wild flowers and columbines, beside cascading water, past Peacock Pool, and along a ridge with an unobstructed view of the forbidding Diamond face. I walked through the shelter-cabin door. The cabin had small bunk beds. Layton was sprawled across the top bunk. Six-foot-four, his legs and arms seemed to spill over the sides of the bed. A sling with a great amount of pitons and carabiners clipped to it was hanging from a crossbeam. Royal stood with his back to me. He was examining the gear. When he turned, I saw a man with glasses and a beard. He was wearing a brown shirt, blue knickers, knee-length red socks, climbing boots called Spiders, and a short-billed, kind of forties, British, motor hat.

What he saw was a high school student. He greeted me warmly, but also with a certain austerity, with a deep voice and handshake. It was late afternoon, and there was a mood that was settling across the mountain.

A major contribution to the spiritual progress of climbing was being made with the attitudes of a group of early Yosemite climbers--Chuck Pratt, Tom Frost, TM Herbert, Joe Fitschen, Dick McCracken, etc., and their give-or-take spiritual leader, Royal Robbins. Everyone in Yosemite who was actively climbing, even a rival of Royal's, or an enemy, or an "indifferent," was affected by him.

This band of Yosemite climbers were keepers of the flame, it might be said, in paying respect to Salathe, Young, Mummery, Buhl, Bonatti, Brown, and other mountaineering predecessors who had tried to preserve the integrity of climbing and who did not use methods that put adventure in jeopardy. The rock was a vehicle not only for the development of styles but also for the liberation of personalities. Royal and company created themselves, as they created climbing for us all. It was as though the development of their souls hinged on their art, a process that was infectious. Their higher level of expertise and their scruples brought a new, independent movement to climbing that captured the imagination of people the world over.

Robbins' spirit, in particular, radiated out from photos--pictorial representations from early *Summit* magazines and an early '60s *American Alpine Journal*. Climbers felt the quiet power of this strong, remote person with a neatly trimmed beard. He wore sunglasses and seemed to stare out from behind those glasses almost darkly into your soul, as though truth, adventure, and perfection were for him an inward necessity and, to get along with him, the same were going to be required of you.

You were going to have to be with him, somehow, in the Vision. He was true to himself. Integrity was at the center of the game, as was he at the center of the young assembly of star climbers. The air of superiority that he could affect or rather at times his Olympian condescension, was, to friends such as Herbert, understandable. Herbert says: "Most of the big breakthroughs came from Royal. I felt that I could probably keep up with most of the other climbers, but I knew I would never equal Royal. Going up on a wall with him was almost like cheating. If anything went wrong, you'd just give him the lead."

A redeeming power of climbing, a quality of its mixed elations and horrors and follies, was that it seemed to lend concrete existence to abstract notions of the spirit of a person. As any worthy enterprise, climbing was the measure of an individual's character and tended to isolate a person--in Royal's example, high up in the super-individual sphere.

He was the master of climbs so serious that at times he had to draw his life out. There were times he shuddered and hoped that there was a next foothold or a fifi-hook placement anywhere ahead for a rest or a re-focus or a wry smile, a degree of climbing that he survived perhaps only because of the ideals that were in the balance.

Oscar Wilde wrote, "all fine imaginative work is self-conscious and deliberate." Royal was following this sort of will-to-art, ideologically brilliant, insightful, driven to be the climber of Yosemite's enormous, statuesque, granite walls. These were walls whose profanation, he would insist, was forbidden and whose magic was somewhat lost by communicating it to others. It was often insinuated snidely that Half Dome or El Capitan could be regarded as Royal's personal property. In his own soft-hued words in later years, Royal would say, "I consider Half Dome my tombstone. Is that grotesquely egoistic?"

Royal was an obvious star, unique, admired, but in another sense solitary--in spite of his countless friends or imitators. As I stood in the door of the dark shelter-cabin, I could feel his aloneness--that mood. It settled over Longs Peak.

On July 11th of '63, Royal and Layton started up into the granite realm of the Diamond--sheer rock colored gold, orange, and yellow as sun rose on it. This would be the third ascent of the Diamond via the original Rearick-Kamps route.

98 Bob Kamps and Dave Rearick, 1960 pioneers of the Diamond -- photo by Glen Prossen

99 Kor leading on the Diamond -- photo by Royal Robbins

I watched Royal and Layton race up the wall. They did it in one breathless day--a very fast ascent for that period in climbing history. Two days later, on the 13th, they pioneered a new route, also in a single day, a line they called the Jack of Diamonds. It paralleled the Rearick-Kamps to the right. Two of the greatest climbers in the world were sharing one rope and were doing something phenomenal. They were making a one-day ascent of a dangerous, mountain wall that before had required two exhausting days broken by a cold night out on a tiny ledge.

The climbing was strenuous, and it was difficult to breathe at an altitude approaching fourteen thousand feet. Royal by no means found it easy to keep up with the rapid pace of Layton Kor. When the sun left the East Face, their fingers were numb from the cold, and snow whirled around them. Royal found himself doing battle with an intense, foot-and-fist jam crack, thirty feet above his piton and straining to hold on. He jammed a hand and foot and hurriedly hammered a piton into a rotten crack. The pin was poor but took the partial support of one foot until he could get a better piton higher.

Later in the book *CLIMB!*, by Bob Godfrey and Dudley Chelton, he spoke of descending from the summit of the Diamond:

"Mile after mile through the night I paced steadily behind Kor, through the Boulder Field--which seemed an enormous area. Kor showed no signs of weakening, and I forced myself to thrust my legs forward, long strides trying to match his. I wouldn't weaken.... Aching feet, legs, back. Mind numbed, but there was the light of the shelter; crowded, sordid, smelly, but warm and welcoming. I remember Liz, but, oddly, I can't recall booze. Ah, I have grown so sophisticated that I can't imagine a climb like that, with a walk like that, not being followed by wine, as well as love."

Either before or between these two ascents of the Diamond, Royal and I put up a four hundred-foot climb called "the Gang Plank" on an overhanging wall above Chasm Lake. He carried a tiny notepad and pen he pulled from his shirt pocket from time to time to record information such as the number of pitches, their grading, and number of pitons we used. He was quiet most of this ascent and led two extremely difficult direct-aid pitches with RURPS and pitons placed only by their tips. A fifi-hook was used on a tiny place of rock, and one utterly unbelievable piton was set into a crack on its side. The blade of this piton didn't touch anything, but the eye of the piton--by some apparent disregard of physical law--rested in a single place atop a crystal. Royal hung from this piton with his full weight, as did I when I followed. When I gingerly transferred my weight to the next piton above, I was able to remove the sensational piton by simply lifting it away from its perch with my hand.

100 Robbins on the Gang Plank, Longs Peak -- photo by Pat Ament

124

101 Remarkable piton placement -- photo by Pat Ament

102 A woman's place is at the shelter cabin (Longs Peak), Liz washes the climbers' dishes (note wrist in cast) -- photo by Royal Robbins

Jim McCarthy managed to get five hundred dollars from the American Alpine Club for the purpose of an alpine ascent in the "Cirque of the Unclimbables" in northwest Canada. McCarthy teamed with Layton Kor, Dick McCracken, and Royal. All four and Liz were squashed into Jim's Volkswagen bug and headed north from Boulder, the tires of the car sticking out from the weight of the five people and their gear. Along the way, they stopped in the Tetons where Royal and Liz climbed the Grand Teton with her wrist in a cast. By the end of the ascent, Liz's cast was in tatters.

103 Liz Robbins on the Grand Teton
-- photo by Royal Robbins

Prior to this trip, she had fallen off a boulder problem done by Janie Taylor at Indian Rock in Berkeley. In thinking back, Liz admitted that she must have felt competitive with Janie, although Janie was, Liz admitted, "a better climber."

Royal left Liz in the Tetons, and the four climbers endured a several-day, flat-tire, and car-trouble-filled drive north. The route of their choice became an eighteen hundred-foot wall in the Logan mountains: the Southeast Face of Mount Proboscis.

104 Layton Kor and Jim McCarthy on the approach to Proboscis --
photo by Royal Robbins

They climbed the wall in three and a half days, from August 4th to the 7th (1963). It was an ominous, Yosemite-like wall in a serious, alpine setting-- but with only six-hour nights. They spent one of those nights hanging in slings. It was a difficult, although elegant, route the climbers later said was characterized by "sophisticated nailing," an ingenuity of piton placements, and one beautiful pitch after another with skyhooks and RURPS.

McCracken recalls: "From the lake that we flew to by float plane, the approach to the Logans was horrendous. With our heavy packs, we kept falling through the muskeg--up to mid-thigh sometimes. It often was easier to walk in the stream we were following rather than alongside it. Royal was lucky, as well as being a good climber. He and I won the toss as to who should lead the first half of the route. It turned out that we got the most interesting half. When we were preparing to leave our camp and return the long distance to the lake for the pickup by the float plane, a survey-party helicopter landed in the meadow next to us to say hello. The pilot came back later and offered to take our packs down for us. Unfortunately for Jim and Layton, they were off on a walk. So the helicopter took only Royal's pack and mine. Jim and Layton were indignant when they returned. The next day, Jim and Layton were in a hurry to leave (since they were carrying packs and we weren't) and departed ahead of Royal and me. About half and hour after they were gone, the helicopter showed up again and offered to give one of us a ride. Royal was lucky again. He won the toss."

105 Upward onto the ever-steepening wall of Proboscis

106 Layton Kor begins to rappel from the summit of Proboscis, Royal and Jim await their turn -- photo by Richard McCracken

Liz hitched a ride back to California, her body stuffed onto the top of packs and climbing gear in the back seat of someone's small car. She had contracted and was knocked flat by a condition she couldn't identify but which turned out to be mononucleosis. She arrived in California and was hospitalized, "exhausted, and wondering what life was all about."

Royal returned to Yosemite and made a probe up the somber, overhanging, Southeast Wall of El Capitan--the North America Wall--in October, with Glen Denny. This wall was named after a large section of black rock roughly the outline of North America. They climbed to the six hundred-foot level of the two thousand-foot wall. But Royal fell, and the rope burned Glen's hands. They retreated.

107 Glen Denny (top) and Royal Robbins on the third pitch of the North America Wall of El Capitan -- photo by Tom Frost

Royal and Liz realized that their future was together and were married November 17th, 1963. They wanted something more than a county clerk so decided to be married in the Church of the New Jerusalem, SwedenBorgain, in San Francisco. It was a place where they felt comfortable, as close to being outside in nature as was possible inside a building, and they were not asked to claim any theological allegiance. They learned, interestingly, that the minister used to be a climber.

108 Liz and Royal

109 What a pair (Liz and Royal Robbins) -- photo by Tom Frost

In May 1964, Royal and Denny decided to make another reconnaissance of the North America Wall of El Cap and went again up on the wall, this time with Tom Frost, in order to push the route a little farther and get some knowledge of what the eventual full-scale attempt might involve. In three days, they climbed to the twelve hundred-foot level, half of the wall, and reached "Big Sur Ledge." On the very difficult third pitch, which before had been led with an array of innovative pitoning tricks in troublesome, incipient cracks, Tom led upward with great speed. Royal recognized this as a level of aid-climbing proficiency that was unrivalled. Royal later wrote, "Tom has a large reservoir of that most important ingredient in alpinism: spirit." Denny remembers Frost: "He was so calm and relaxed. It was as though he didn't know we were off the ground. 'Tom, the plane has left.'" Denny adds, "Frost would take photos in places no other climber would want to. He would never let anything discourage him from taking photos. In the most precarious situations, or where another climber might think the camera was buried too deeply in the pack, he would go ahead and dig it out and shoot. No climber has produced such a fine collection of photos from such remarkable places."

110 Robbins on the second recon of the North America Wall of El Cap -- photo by Tom Frost

111 Glen Denny -- photo by Tom Frost

112 Robbins, more
note-taking
-- photo by Tom Frost

113 Robbins
-- photo by Tom Frost

114 North America Wall, Robbins looking for a route -- photo by Tom Frost

115 Robbins makes a pendulum
above the Valley floor
-- photo by Tom Frost

The climbers encountered challenge after challenge and, on the fourth day of climbing, rappelled to the ground. As Royal prepared the last rappel, two tiny frogs crept from a crack and "cavorted happily" on the anchor pitons.

Royal did a major ascent in June, the second ascent of the West Buttress of El Capitan--a line Kor and Roper had pioneered. Royal went with Pratt, after two attempts with other people where "things went wrong." He and Kamps, for example, had gotten off route and ended up going too slow. Royal and Kamps decided that, even though they knew they could get up the route, it wasn't going to be the elegant ascent Royal wanted it to be.

136 136136

136

116 Chuck Pratt on the West Buttress of El Capitan -- photo by Royal Robbins

Also in June, Royal and Tom Frost made a continuous ascent of the Dihedral Wall of El Capitan. The pioneers of this route, including the "outsider" Ed Cooper, had fixed ropes to nineteen hundred feet, once more, in Royal's view, a first ascent of a major route in Yosemite done using the old methods of expeditionary rock climbing that had in Yosemite, Royal felt, been put to sleep. He asked in another of his writings, "What fun is there in a game when the odds are a hundred to one in your favor?" For Royal, climbing turned on the idea of human character, the soul, the heart, the spirit.

117 Robbins, sunlit rock, the Dihedral Wall of El Cap -- photo by Tom Frost

118 Robbins on the Dihedral Wall -- photo by Tom Frost

119 Frost frowns at bolts -- photo by Royal Robbins

120 Frost, bivouac in net hammock, Dihedral Wall of El Cap
  -- photo by Royal Robbins

1 Robbins tries to wake up, morning, hammock bivouac, Dihedral Wall of El Cap
-- photo by Tom Frost

122 Frost follows an exposed pitch on the Dihedral Wall -- photo by Royal Robbins

123 Tom Frost -- photo by Royal Robbins

On the Dihedral Wall and West Buttress routes, Royal introduced to the climbing world the more refined, efficient methods that could be enjoyed with the use of jumar prusik handles, including the double jumar/pulley system--for bringing up the heavy haul bag. This system made hauling vastly easier, and the speed of an ascent could be increased with the second man jumaring a pitch at the same time the leader hauled the bag. These would become the chosen methods for thousands of big-wall climbers to come.

124 Joe Fitschen at the top of El Capitan, to greet Robbins and Frost after the Dihedral Wall -- photo by Harry Daley

One day in Yosemite, Royal, Liz, and Frost were sitting around Royal's site in Camp 4, at a picnic table. They were outwardly meditating on life. The gist of their talk was to ask what was worthwhile in life, or more worthwhile than climbing. Royal said, in so many words, that climbing was largely what life was about for him. He basically didn't see anything more valuable at the time than climbing. Frost had no rebuttal. Liz smiled with feminine intuition, not in complete agreement.

VII

A huge rock wall called Hooker, in the Wind River Range of Wyoming was unclimbed and next on the ongoing masterpiece agenda of Royal Robbins. It was July of '64, and his partners were Dick McCracken and Charlie Raymond. Liz came with them, as did a few other friends. McCracken, Raymond, and Robbins prefaced Hooker with the first complete traverse of the "Cirque of the Towers," from Pingora to Warbonnet. This took a little over a day. And on July 18th, Charlie and Royal made the first ascent of the eight hundred-foot South Buttress of Watchtower. This was an impressive wall in the Cirque of the Towers area and took a long day, in rain and lightning.

Beginning July 22nd and finishing noon July 25th, with three nights on the wall, McCracken, Raymond, and Robbins then climbed the eighteen hundred-foot North Face of Mount Hooker. The first seven hundred feet required two days and the use of eight fifi-hooks, the weather cold and windy.

125 Charlie Raymond on "nested" pitons, Mt. Hooker -- photo by Royal Robbins

126 Richard McCracken leans out to study the wall
-- photo by Royal Robbins

144

127 Robbins tries to wake up, morning, after hammock bivouac on Hooker
-- photo by Richard McCracken

128 Royal still in bed on Hooker (contrary to popular opinion, he did not sleep the entire ascent) -- photo by Richard McCracken

129 Charlie Raymond leading on the fourth morning, Hooker
-- photo by Richard McCracken

Royal later wrote in an article of the "rape" sheep had rendered to whole hillsides in the area, turning grassy slopes into "sand dunes."

It was not far from the Wind Rivers to the Needles of South Dakota. Royal and Liz climbed for a week or so in August in the Needles where spires standing in mountain forests provided small but formidable challenges. While climbing many of the established classic routes, Royal pioneered a few first ascents. "Cerberus," for example, became "an all-time classic," as stated in the area guidebook. With Liz, Dick Laptad, and Sue Prince, Royal led the first free ascent of "Queenpin." And, belayed by Liz, he led the first ascent of "Incisor."

130 Royal in the Needles

It takes genius to recognize genius, and Royal was awed by the incredibly challenging, short climbs done in the Needles by John Gill. Largely dismissed by other climbers as a freak of bouldering, Gill had climbed the thirty-foot North Overhang of the Thimble entirely without protection--no rope, no spot. He had employed only nerve, mentality, technique, and finger-arm strength far beyond that of any other climber. Royal was not able to repeat the Thimble route and was unwilling to demean it by attempting it with a top-rope--that wasn't playing the game. Finding a different route up, Royal wrote in the summit register: "Hats off to John Gill."

131 Royal attempting Gill's
    route on the Thimble

132 The Human Fly, John Gill, on "the Scab," in the Needles

Devils Tower, the monolith rising high out of Wyoming's northeast plains, was an unavoidable stop for Royal and Liz. On August 19th, 1964, he led the first ascent of Danse Macabre (rated 5.10d, i.e. extreme) and on August 10th the Window Route with Pete Robinson--a student at Colorado State University. The Window Route, up the East Face of the tower, involved seven or eight hundred feet of difficult climbing. Rain and sleet during the final two hours of the ascent, including a fifteen-foot overhang near the top, made things even more difficult.

Royal led the historic "Wiessner Crack," using only one piton for protection--as had the great pioneer climber Fritz Wiessner. Royal wished to respect the bold style of Wiessner's feat. Royal also found himself leading "Gooseberry Jam." This was recommended to him by Bob Kamps and was reported to be one of the hardest cracks on Devils Tower. Royal had to try it. But the route led up through what he recognized as other than "Gooseberry." He completed the "sandbag" test piece at the cost of a case of poison ivy.

Then Royal and Liz returned to Colorado. He and I made several first or first free ascents in Eldorado Canyon and Boulder Canyon. We did the first free ascent of the classic "Yellow Spur" in Eldorado, a six hundred-foot lovely, yellow-green buttress rising to a sharp peak. When he led the vertical crux, Royal walked up it as though it were something for beginners.

A few hard pulls on small finger holds were required to do the first ascent of the "Final Exam" on Castle Rock in Boulder Canyon.

Royal led an evil-looking, overhanging chimney-crack near Final Exam that he named with one of his puns: By Gully. There had been bolt wars on the initial blank wall of Country Club Crack, and Royal showed how the face could be aid-climbed using no bolts at all. He then lowered back to the start and, with a top-rope, quite easily free-climbed the pitch his first try. The current rating of this stretch of rock is the very difficult 5.11+! I followed the pitch free, and Royal led up the rest of the route without aid except for one or two points at the very top of the route. His effort on this climb was groundwork for the eventual free ascent that would be made by other climbers three years later.

133 Royal leading the Final Exam in Boulder Canyon, Colorado
-- photo by Judy Rearick

Another climb on Castle Rock, given the name "Athlete's Feat" by Royal, pushed a new level of boldness. An undercling-lieback to an overhang, a delicate move up to the top edge of the overhang, and then an intangible mantel onto a slanting shelf were combined with the danger of a possible fall fifteen feet back down onto a large spike of rock. A few years later, the route became protected when a couple of beginning aid-climbers thought they were doing a new route up a wall impossible without bolts. They placed two bolts in the pitch. Subsequent climbers compromised and removed the first bolt but kept the second one--still happily used to this day by the best of climbers. The bolt eliminated the danger of the fall onto the spike of rock.

It remains that Royal led the first ascent of that route without the bolt and relied on ability to rise to the challenge of a climb, rather than reducing the difficulty by the use of a bolt. Many people felt in the '60s that this first pitch of Athlete's Feat (there were four other difficult pitches above) was the most demanding free-climbing in the country--aside from John Gill's bouldering routes.

While in Colorado, Royal teamed with Dave Rearick and Dan Davis for the second ascent of Layton Kor and Paul Mayrose's notorious, horrific-looking fissure in Estes Park, the "Crack Of Fear," on the Twin Owls. Slicing for two hundred and fifty feet up a steep wall of rock, the Crack Of Fear involved Yosemite-like "off-width" techniques. The crack was slippery and overhanging in places and often too wide to place protection--but too narrow for the body to fit far enough into to be secure. Despite eliminating all but one point of the direct-aid used by the first ascent party, Royal led the climb in shorts! Without the protection of long pants to keep from scraping his knees against the rough rock inside the crack, the pain was a factor--it undoubtedly made the climbing more difficult. Royal was not one to turn away from a test, nor would he allow an error in judgment to translate into defeat.

With Bob Beal, Royal led the first free ascent of another difficult crack in the Estes Park area, called "Turnkorner," on Sundance Buttress. A couple of falls were required before Royal mastered the crux--an overhanging, flared slot.

Royal, Liz, and I went to Split Rocks, west of Lyons, Colorado, a bouldering area where we tried our abilities and Royal posed for photos for a climbing instruction book he was writing. It would later be called *Basic Rockcraft*, a small book that would sell over two hundred thousand copies.

In September, when Royal and Liz felt it was time to begin migrating toward Yosemite, they invited me to go with them. It would mean a few side trips along the way, including a stop in Salt Lake City for a climbing seminar and possibly some climbing on the red, desert rock of Utah. We would stay a night at their Sugar Bowl chalet at the top of a Sierra pass in California.

I was a summer out of high school, with the first ascent of a new route on the Diamond under my belt. In my mind, I was already in Yosemite. I had the warm encouragement of my parents. At a dinner my mother prepared before we left on the trip, Royal said to her, "This is not just a meal, it is an experience." Here was the generous, easy-going Robbins, the one that would bring a bottle of champagne to his friends.

It seemed at other times that Royal and Liz had some grandiose idea about themselves. Royal was a man who selected his words, and your saying too much could produce a quick stare. Cocky and confident, Royal's attitude was to do the hardest climbs that existed in whatever area at the time. Liz was not easy to read and sometimes put people off with what came across as smug self-assurance. Climbers trying to get at Royal took swipes at Liz. She was characterized as adoring of Royal, was said to swoon at his every assertion. Liz did leave a feeling with a small number of people in Boulder, Colorado, that her upbringing was a jot better than theirs. After a dinner that Royal and Liz were invited to at Heidi and Paul Mayrose's house, Heidi offered the story that Liz lifted and examined a dish at the start of dinner, curious of the dish's material. To Heidi, Liz was categorizing the social class of the Mayroses. This was perhaps Heidi's perception (she was temperamental) rather than Liz's intent, for Liz might not have chosen to be with Royal if she truly cared what people had in the way of material possessions.

Royal and Liz were a study for me, along our trip, and I became the occasional subject of their play. Now and then my two mentors aroused my defenses. It seemed that just by his looking at you...already you had failed a test or two. Every day, however, also brought an abundance of the best feelings. One could tolerate the imperfections or the twinges of snobbery. These were mixed with friendship and happiness and new places that we went. Royal was full of puns. When I complained of a sore muscle, he replied that I didn't have to get sore about it. When he was holding a zucchini in a supermarket, he blurted, "Gee, mom, isn't the zoo keeny?" Royal's plays on words had a supportive, brilliant side, for example his "Layton the Great 'n"--in tribute to Layton Kor.

We drove to northwestern New Mexico and climbed Shiprock.

134 Royal walks toward Shiprock from camp near lone boulder
-- photo by Pat Ament

135 Royal leading the crux wall near the top of Shiprock
-- photo by Pat Ament

136 Liz Robbins at the summit of Shiprock -- photo by Royal Robbins

The route up Shiprock, including the ascent and descent, covered six thousand feet of volcanic rhyolite, tuff-breccia, and basalt. On this climb, I recall feeling a real sense of comradeship with Royal and Liz.

She was willing to relinquish the leading to Royal and me but was by no means simply a follower. She climbed every difficult move on rock that we did. Women in the early 1960's were not viewed as being able to climb what men could. She was showing us that such presumptions were due for revision. Because she didn't have as much arm strength as we, she often made up for it with resourceful technique--always scanning the rock for the foothold that would save arm strength.... Most of the time, it seemed that she was less afraid than I.

The ghastly, huge, red formation of Shiprock, rising out of hundreds of square miles of flat desert, had an eerie, ghostly, and lonely feel about it that latched onto the depths and darknesses of our minds.

Starting late in the day and getting to the top just before dark, we had little time to contemplate the boundless view of desert in all directions and descended first in twilight and then in starlight. The rappels, the traverses that had to be reversed, and the strong, supernatural feeling of being lost up in the black, windblown reaches of this formation, were experienced in a kind of reach-in-the-dark way.

Liz and I were assured in the company of this wizard who had his own will. He was confident, and we believed that we would bring ourselves down alive. Royal described Shiprock as a "labyrinthine palace of Satan." It was not as diabolical as that but rather was a beautiful maelstrom with its wind and starlight. There was the smell of dark, brown-red rock and the air of the ancient desert. We descended with little conversation, listening to patterns of wind against the rock or the sound of rope as it scraped softly against an edge of rock. In the far distance was the sound of tom-toms. It was a searching of illusory appearances, for sight and touch.

After midnight at our camp at the bottom by an isolated boulder in the prairie, in a desolate, breezy, quiet, tired, carefree night under the full firmament, we celebrated with a steak dinner.

Climbing was, to use Royal's word differently, the labyrinth of one's being. Because he recognized the splendors, Royal did not shrink from the dangers. The joyous, artistic life was in part a fight for the soul's freedom.

158

137 Pat Ament is handed an egg on toast for breakfast, the morning
after Shiprock -- photo by Royal Robbins

The five hundred-foot, red Castleton Tower near Moab, Utah, was being
struck by lightning. It was raining, so we decided to drive along an unknown dirt
road and explore the sage-covered hills of the desert. As we drove up a hill, the
green Mercedes that had been given to Royal and Liz as a wedding present was
suddenly stuck in mushy, deep, cement-like clay. Liz took charge of the steering
wheel, while Royal and I attempted to stack rocks under the wheels for traction.
We succeeded, by a miracle. As the car started to move, Royal and I jumped
inside--covered to the elbows in wet mud. We then realized we were almost out
of gas and miles from nowhere. By a stroke of fortune, we were able to coast
downhill about fifteen miles to a gas station.

The next day, Castleton Tower rose into cloudless sky. The tower had
been climbed only twice before. Once again Liz and I were caught up in Royal's
confidence and began upward through the crimson, plant-filled washes and up the
slides of scree leading to the striking sandstone tower. It looked like a high,
ruby-purple building sitting atop a fabulous cone of shattered, red rubble.

Starting late again and finishing just at dark again, we could only briefly
enjoy the view of pink-yellow terrain that extended in all directions as the sun
set. The several rappels in darkness made us feel again joined in some valuable,
ghostly adventure.

VIII

Royal, Liz, and I camped and hiked for a couple of days among the unusual rock configurations of Arches National Monument. One night by camplight, Royal and I bouldered on a red slab. I managed a "no-hands" route where the soft sandstone crumbled away slightly under my shoes, and there was not enough of a foothold left for Royal to be able to do the problem.

38 Grapes suddenly appear in Royal's ear and mouth -- photo by Pat Ament

At Rich Ream's house, where we stayed in Salt Lake, we listened to Dvorzak's New World Symphony and to Bob Dylan. I didn't understand what I was supposed to see in Dylan, until his individuality and lyrical genius were explained to me by Royal. In the next few years, I would become almost obsessed with Dylan--in part a statement of the power Royal had to influence my life.

In Salt Lake's Little Cottonwood Canyon, Royal fell onto a pointed stump while bushwhacking down through a jumble of trees. The stump punctured the back of his leg, near the top of his thigh. At the Ream residence, Royal struggled to keep from fainting. I sat quietly near him in the kitchen, as Liz and Rich kept an eye on him. I was somewhat stunned and wished that I could help. For the first time, I began to realize that Royal was human, that he was vulnerable. Royal's repugnance was magnified when a doctor probed the puncture with a finger.

139 Royal uses chimney techniques in a flared crack
in Little Cottonwood Canyon, Utah

But the climbing seminar in Salt Lake had to go on. I served as a type of assistant instructor as Royal showed his manteling and footwork skills on a large boulder. The students were captivated all day. He aided a big overhang for them, and they studied his every move on rock.

As we drove into the Sierra Nevada toward Sugar Bowl, Royal pointed out the first occurrences of solid, white, Sierra granite. He was astute in his sense of the beautiful, observing the character and varied moods and tranquility of the Sierra. He was watchful of beauty as he climbed, letting the serenity of El

Capitan and the grandeur of the Yosemite surroundings permeate him. A whole generation of climbing was being molded, to a degree, by the power of his perceptions, and the climbing world was finding--or at least remembering--its values, as he openly communicated his.

There was a freshness in the early '60s, brought in part by Royal. He looked at nature, the serene Sierra trees, the rivers, the sky, and storms. He was magic, in the style of the venerated photographer Ansel Adams, enacting for us a vision of the world.

At the same time, it was difficult to feel at ease with Royal. I felt I had to be better than myself. My technique at thought, as well as climbing, had to be sharper than it was normally. He was competitive but not mean-spirited. He was good-humored. You wanted to oblige this difficult, mysterious man who, unfortunately, had the astuteness to divine your intentions. He would, without warning, turn mocking or cynical. He would question your logic. Small talk, attempts at polite conversation, sometimes went unreciprocated. But the techniques that you expressed later on rock, out of the presence of his company, the things you said that had his voice, were a mark of his example in your life, a mark of his friendship, a pride that you felt in knowing him.

Imagine being introduced to Yosemite by Royal, of all people. What a blessing! We drove first into the high country of Tuolumne and spent a night in a meadow below the stars. Royal pointed out constellations--Orion, Cassiopeia.... In the morning, dew covered our sleeping bags. We drove eagerly down through the enormous sugar pines and red fir, along the curving road, into Yosemite Valley. I will never forget my first view of El Capitan. I was looking for something smaller, or at least less big, but then it was suddenly there before us and taking up an unexpectedly large portion of the sky.

We went to breakfast at the lodge cafeteria where we happened onto Chuck Pratt. Royal introduced us. Then it was off to a short first ascent along the base of Glacier Point Apron, a 5.10 friction pitch Royal led without hesitation. "Lizard," Royal's affectionate occasional name for Liz, also climbed the route. The next day, Royal led me up an overhanging, flared, 5.10 crack at the base of El Capitan. He was in extraordinary command of the techniques required to lead such a crack, and I learned by emulating those techniques.

He then introduced me to Chris Fredericks and suggested that Chris and I climb the North Face of Sentinel. It was autumn of 1964, and Royal wanted no delay in my furthering my apprenticeship.

During this month in Yosemite, Royal climbed the fifteen hundred-foot West Face of Sentinel Rock with Yvon Chouinard for filmmakers Roger Brown and Tom Frost. During a spell before filming, a number of ropes were fixed down the wall that would aid the photo crew. A brash, young man named Tom Cochrane had the idea of using these ropes to get an easy peek at the West Face route. He hiked up the backside and began to rappel down the ropes from the top. But not all of the ropes were in place, and he found himself part way down the wall, on a stance, with no equipment with which to prusik back up. He was forced to spend a cold, embarrassing bivouac. When someone reported Cochrane's plan and that he was missing, Royal, Pratt, Frost, and I walked up toward Sentinel in the dark. Pratt and I waited at the start of the angling "Tree Ledge" while Royal and Frost groped upward along the ledge in blackness to the start of the West Face route. They yelled up into the darkness, but wind blew the sounds of their voices away. They heard nothing in the way of a response. It was too dark for anything to be done. The next morning, Royal and Frost hiked the slabby, tedious ravine up the backside of Sentinel to the summit, began to rappel, and after a short distance found the cold, stranded climber.

IX

By mid-October, 1964, Yosemite was still enjoying warm weather. Plans were brewing for an all-out ascent of the North America Wall of El Capitan. Tom Frost and Chuck Pratt were ready. Chouinard had been invited as a fourth although was not yet in Yosemite. Royal said that I could take Chouinard's place if he didn't show. When Chouinard arrived, I was secretly disappointed and decided that it was at last time for me to leave Yosemite and return to Colorado. While I was riding freight trains home, Robbins, Pratt, Frost, and Chouinard were on the North America Wall.

140 The North America Wall of El Capitan -- photo by Tom Frost

The treacherous, black diorite, the difficulty of retreat due to great overhangs and long traverses, the obvious difficult climbing and aid challenges, and the absence of a natural line along cracks made this wall a most foreboding undertaking. Chouinard took a short fall and was caught by a RURP. Frost took a short fall when a tiny horn supporting an aid sling broke. He passed the difficulty with the use of a hook.

High on the wall, they lowered Tom sixty feet from a bolt. This placed him almost level with them, but thirty feet away. Using a separate rope to his waist, they pulled him to them and then let go. Tom pendulumed far away, reaching a flake otherwise inaccessible.

141 Robbins (distant) and Pratt traverse toward the bottom of the Black Dihedral -- photo by Tom Frost

They climbed after dark, a pattern that would become familiar throughout the climb.

On the fifth day on the wall, they found themselves in the nightmarish, dirty, and overhanging "Black Dihedral." It was huge, blotted out the sky, had loose rock, and leaned oppressively to the right for several hundred feet.

142 Robbins at a hanging belay, approaching the start of the Black Dihedral -- photo by Tom Frost

143 Looking down out of the Black Dihedral -- photo by Tom Frost

By the end of the sixth day, they reached the overhang at the top of the dihedral, hammered pitons in, attached their hammocks, and spent a foreboding night under the overhang, suspended over space, one above another over a great void, "like laundry between tenement flats," as Royal wrote. They had painted themselves so far up into a corner and into such a mentally anguishing position that it was hard to believe that this would also have to be their home for the night. From Frost's perspective, "Royal had the audacity to string his hammock free, between two opposing walls, so that one side of his body would not have to lean against the rock. I was too oppressed at the view of the exposure to think of such a thing." By flashlight, Tom observed large centipedes crawling on the ceiling of rock above his head. During the night, guitarist and singer Mort Hempel serenaded the climbers with rare, beautiful folk songs through a small two-way radio Royal had decided to bring.

The real fright didn't occur until the sun came up and, after a yawn and opening their eyes, they saw where they were--dangling sixteen hundred feet above the ground.

144 Top to bottom: Tom Frost, Royal Robbins, Yvon Chouinard, "laundry between tenement flats," at the hanging bivouac beneath the overhang at the top of the Black Dihedral -- photo by Chuck Pratt

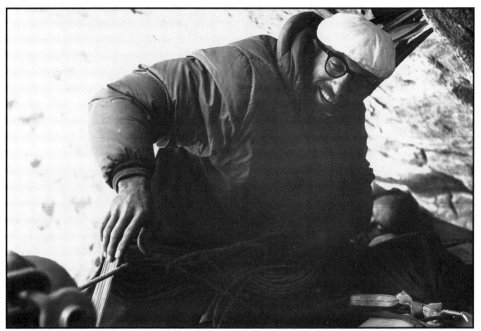

145 Robbins makes light of the situation, at the hammock bivouac -- photo by Tom Frost

Ken Wilson, British editor, reflects about these four climbers:

"The big four--Robbins, Pratt, Frost, and Chouinard--together seemed to exert a very strong moral force, Pratt silent and brilliant, Frost cheerful, humble, and friendly, yet with that religious dignity, Chouinard impish, quite sharp and critical yet skillful, a great trend-setter, and Robbins an almost Buddha-like presence, a supreme dignity tinged with courage to say and do controversial things, a sort of moral leadership in both words as well as deeds. Royal could see that any idiot could bolt his way up a big wall. The great Yosemite routes are not mindless bolt-ladders but really tenuous exercises in the just-possible. There is little doubt that without the core of Yosemite activists in the early 1960's, and I would include Sacherer and Kor as part of the group, America would have been a far less ethical place, climbingwise, in the last thirty years."

Clouds began to appear. Pratt drove pitons straight up in a crack under the overhang as he traversed outward to the right.

146 Mind over matter, Pratt finds a way out the overhang
-- photo by Tom Frost

170

Then he pitoned over and above the overhang. From here, with only the upper part of his body above the overhang, he traversed thirty feet back left. The other climbers watched the lower part of Pratt's body inch sideways, horizontally across their line of view, in space behind them. They studied their predicament, as this bewildering climb continued to unfold. Piton placements were difficult. At last Pratt ended the pitch, hanging in slings. Royal called Pratt's achievement "the most spectacular lead in American climbing."

Short, solid, powerful Chuck Pratt turned difficult rock into art. He was remarkable also in that he rejected any opportunity to cash in on his fame. Patient, a good sense of humor, he climbed because he loved to. There was no hidden agenda. He valued the solitude and the friendship and the experience. As with Royal, Pratt's love for Yosemite went deep into the trees and into the greens of the rivers and into the mystical experience of such wonders. Pratt had quit college and become a kind of society dropout. He drank beer a lot and seemed to suffer quietly from inner torments he was not willing to share. Yet on the most difficult crack climbs, with no protection and looking at a death fall, or on the most spectacular lead in American climbing, he was imperturbable.

147 Chuck Pratt -- photo by Tom Frost

In Camp 4 one night, Pratt drank beer and then in army boots climbed a new, virtually unrepeatable, lichen-covered route up the smooth Columbia Boulder. He could be found juggling wine bottles or heard in a fit of laughter. Sometimes in Camp 4, there were delirious shouts that came out of the dark. He could be sullen, distant, irritable, or, in moments of repose, gentle and obliging. Pratt had an adversary in a bear by the name of Spartacus. Pratt was known for his bad luck with Yosemite bears who on more than one occasion molested his tent or belongings. He and Spartacus knew each other like clockwork. There was a mutual respect, but while Pratt was imperturbable... Spartacus was an immovable mountain.

Through the tiny, two-way radio, Liz reported that a storm was forecast. Frost and Pratt hated the radio. It intruded into their isolation and into their world. Pratt was a man of great stoicism and did not usually voice his discomforts, but, like Frost, he did not enjoy the daily news reports. It detracted from the climb to have anyone else "with them."

When Chouinard jumared up the overhang, Frost lowered him slowly outward into space to prevent a horrifying, inglorious swing.

148 Chouinard is lowered out from under the overhang, to begin jumaring --
photo by Tom Frost

149 Chouinard jumars past the overhang, Merced River below -- photo by Tom Frost

Frost then lowered himself out and jumared up, spinning on the rope in despair above the void. When Frost arrived at the hanging belay above the overhang, Pratt and Robbins were already a distance up the wall. They were racing up persistently difficult rock, trying, before it stormed, to reach the shelter of a huge recess called "the Cyclop's Eye."

The Cyclop's Eye was an enormous, macabre depression in the wall, like a great curved room with a sloping floor. It afforded refuge. Rain began, and they tied themselves in for the night. The storm hit for real and lashed them with wind and rain.

150 Clouds "like sharks racing after their prey" -- photo by Tom Frost

151 View toward Sentinel from the Cyclop's Eye --
photo by Tom Frost

The climbers had come up hundreds of feet of overhanging rock, and there were hundreds of feet yet above--no turning back. Snow now was all around, and they were cut off from everything. Later in an article about the North America Wall, Royal wrote: "Mankind is truly insignificant. Man's fate, indeed, is to have to swallow these truths and still live on."

These climbers in fact did not feel insignificant. They felt endowed with power, and wherever that power came from, they let it take them, upward, into harrowing places.

The storm unexpectedly turned northeast and broke in the morning, sparing them several days of rain or snow. The difficulties of the climbing continued.

Royal hand-traversed left from Chuck's hanging belay. Chuck then lowered Royal from a sling on a horn. Royal reached around a corner and started pitoning ("nailing") upward beneath a curving arch. The crack was stubborn, "accepting pitons grudgingly." He moved upward on RURPS, knifeblades, and tips of angles, slipping on the moss-covered rock. Ice water ran down his arms and legs. At the top of the arch, a sling through a hole in a flake and then a skyhook got him on his way hand-traversing left again. He was forced, after twenty feet, to stop and hurriedly place a piton. Then he nailed straight left another twenty feet. The exposure was terrifying. At the end of the traverse, he got a knifeblade behind a dubious flake. A skyhook on a tiny ledge allowed him to move five feet higher....

They reached the top six hours into the ninth day, October 31st, 1964, having used only thirty-eight bolts for the entire wall. The weather had cleared. The air was crisp and clean. The summit of El Cap was white, as were the high Sierra mountains to the east.

One thing Royal liked about first ascents was that the notable mountaineering journals had to publish his writings. In his account of the North America Wall climb, in the 1965 *American Alpine Journal*, Royal indulged himself and produced some rather bad writing, an essay full of overblown phrasings that reeked of insincerity and self-consciousness. For not applying the spiritual rigor to his writing that he applied to his climbing, he paid the price of wicked lampooning by his friends as well as by enemies. They ridiculed his melodrama: "We climbed onward, searching, always searching." Awkward passages seemed to come from the head rather than the heart: "...the apparent necessity for many bolts rendered us not happily enthusiastic...." There was an occasional grammatical error: "Six hours later we had overcome the last problems and shook hands on top...." And there were lines that were simply weak: "Next morning, nature smiled." Yet because of the astonishing qualities of the climb, and because a lot of the writing was good, the article was a classic.

Richard Goldstone, a climber from the eastern United States who was a friend and admirer of Royal's, pretended one night around a Yosemite campfire to be playing a violin as he recited lines from memory from Royal's *American Alpine Journal* article: "...menacing clouds, like sharks racing after their prey, scudded toward us..." and "...the rock was dwarfed by the air moving out of the Pacific, and this same storm was just a small blotch on the earth's surface. The earth in turn would be a mere dot on the sun, and there are suns many thousands of times larger than that fiery orb giving us life. If one could only find meaning to make these hard truths of insignificance and omnipresent death acceptable...." Actually such writing wasn't that bad, but it was humorous to hear it put in this context--so unfaithful to Royal. Around a campfire in the Needles of South Dakota, Goldstone was accompanied by a real violinist, Beverly Powell, who pulled her violin from its case as Rich recited Royal's words in the company of Rearick, Kamps, Gill, and others.

As though it were necessary to lessen the mystique of Royal Robbins, climbers found ways of playfully taking him down. They made fun of his first name. I heard Kor, for example, refer to Royal as "the king." People fastened to the bird imagery that was evoked by Royal's last name. In articles of my own, I referred to Royal as "that brown, red-breasted bird of the thrush family" and described him as "winging up" a stretch of rock. I spoke of being "under his wing."

People felt uncomfortable with Royal's all-presence in Yosemite, the way he would size you up, how he would look at you with a cold glance as though you had not yet proven yourself. People questioned the basis of his intellectual pride. The answer was that Royal was intelligent. He studied. He embraced literature, from Shakespeare to Whitman to Sartre to the Lord of the Rings.... One reason for his discourses on man's insignificance was that he was thoughtful and introspective...and alive. He was deeply influenced by Emerson's masterpiece, *Self-Reliance*. At the beginning of that essay are several verses of Beaumont and Fletcher: "Man is his own star; and the soul that can / Render an honest and a perfect man / Commands all light, all influence, all fate...."

Royal had become convinced that the surest path to success in life lay in the development of character and spirit, and that the best way to acquire such attributes was through an adherence to timeless principles. Emerson himself had said, "Nothing finally brings us happiness in life except the triumph of principles." Thus the great works came alive for Royal, in words such as courage, loyalty, trust, fidelity, friendship, love, humor, generosity, tenacity, and resolution. Although he would admit that he often did not live up to these ideals, he honored them. And they became a guide and gave him strength.

178

Tom Higgins, a climber with several such Emersonian qualities, was a natural target of Royal's interest since Tom was obviously a fine artist of footwork and rivaled by no one in terms of honesty of style.

152 Tom Higgins pontificates-- photo by Pat Ament

Tom had "charmed" a way up several very difficult face climbing routes at Tahquitz Rock and in Yosemite. The competition between Royal and Higgins was subtle but noticeable. Royal wrote to me about repeating Higgins' route "Jonah" on Tahquitz. Royal did the route with Liz.

153 Royal leading "Jonah" at Tahquitz Rock

Tom and Royal argued about how climbs were to be graded. Royal wanted gradings to reflect the seriousness and continuousness of the climbing, whereas Higgins thought that only the most difficult single move of a climb should be taken into account. On a nasty pitch of Royal's, called "El Camino Real," at Tahquitz, Higgins took a long fall. Higgins was a 5.11 climber but fell off this route after rating it 5.8. It seemed, to Royal, a delicious irony. Despite the ways Royal and Higgins disagreed, they maintained an impeccable respect for one another.

Out of the sense of Royal's prominence, Sheridan Anderson, a brilliant caricaturist, began to publish delightful cartoons of Royal wearing Superman outfits and asking himself, "Are there no more worlds to conquer?" Friends and enemies alike exulted in Sheridan's comic studies of Royal's pretentiousness, and so did Royal. Sheridan chronicled the personalities of many noted climbers and was able to render a person with precise, satirical strokes. Royal and climbers in general needed to take themselves less seriously. The revelation was heaven sent.

X

Royal was invited by *Summit Magazine* in January of 1965 to serve as rock climbing editor and began to produce a regular flow of writings and philosophical commentaries. He was full of climbing. Even his setbacks provoked philosophical cud-chewings in print, such as in May of '65 failing to figure out the crux move while following the master crack climber Chuck Pratt up the last pitch of the Left Side of "the Slack."

John Harlin, an American climber living in Leysin, Switzerland, had started the "International School of Modern Mountaineering" and was also the sports director for the American School in Leysin--a high school for American kids in Europe, with over two hundred students. Harlin invited Royal to come over and participate. Royal and Liz did not have a lot of money, and would be pushing it to try to afford such a trip, but were not going to turn down the possibilities of this adventure. When they arrived in June of '65, they were taken by the beautiful position of Leysin--high on a mountainside in a lovely alpine setting above Lake Geneva. Royal and Liz resided in a cozy apartment. It was a home base--something Royal didn't have his first trip to Europe. There were no supermarkets in Leysin, only a petite grocery, a bakery, and a meat market, all a short distance away. The apartment had no refrigerator. Thus, before each meal, either Liz or Royal would trundle down through the snow to all of the little shops.

From August 10th to the 13th, 1965, Royal and Harlin made the first ascent of the Direct West Face of the Petit Dru--the great rock face above Chamonix, near Mont Blanc. Part way up the route, Harlin was hit in the thigh by a falling rock. He later wrote in an *American Alpine Journal* account, "Here is where, if Royal were not so eminently qualified for this kind of climbing, there would be but one decision--to go down." Royal was forced to do all the leading, including a stretch of loose rock--one of the most dangerous pitches of his experience. Successive skyhook moves were used to avoid placing pitons that would dislodge huge blocks and flakes.

155 John Harlin on the Dru -- photo by Royal Robbins

During the ascent, a helicopter hovered near the wall to allow a photographer to get some dramatic shots. The photographer later complained that all of his photos were sabotaged. In every photo the climber (Royal) was taking pictures of the photographer.

Royal felt that Harlin was a great alpinist but also was overly enthusiastic about publicity, unlike Hemming or Pratt who seemed almost to desire obscurity. Royal's attitude was perhaps halfway between Harlin's and Pratt's. He wanted the respect of his peers--but let other people recognize you, and deserve it.

Near the summit, a storm began to rage and dropped six inches of snow. With a small two-way radio, they had gotten word back of Harlin's injury. Lito Tejada-Flores and Bev Clark started up the descent route with hopes of assisting the climbers. Lito remembers: "We went up late at night, walked up the tracks of the Montenvers train, under the Dru, then started climbing. Conditions were terrible, with wet wind, and low visibility, but when we reached Royal and John, who had made the summit and were on their way down, John was doing better. They didn't seem to need much help. It was more of a cheerful thing to meet them. The rock was very rotten and was covered with snow. Harlin and I were comfortable on this sort of terrain, but Royal was less relaxed. He did well, but he moved deliberately and with an acute awareness of the danger. On the way down, we bivouacked in the storm. I remember brewing some tea...."

In a postcard to a friend in America, Royal wrote that the descent was more dangerous than the climb--"...lots of loose rock."

Royal also climbed with Chris Bonington, ascending the Grand Mirroir on the Argentine--a huge limestone cliff near Leysin. Bonington remembers, "I was incredibly impressed at how bloody good he was at bouldering. He was absolutely brilliant."

Harlin quit the summer climbing school and his directorship of the American School in order to plan and attempt a winter ascent of the dangerous, six thousand-foot, alpine face of the Eiger. Royal was invited to take over in September as sports director. He and Liz would mainly teach climbing and skiing. Harlin was a charismatic individual, with a lot of skill and energy, but was disorganized. Royal found the records at the American School to be in shambles or nonexistent. It caused a few bad feelings between him and Harlin.

"Liz is my principal sports assistant," Royal wrote in a letter to his mother. And in a letter dated November 25, 1965, he wrote: "Dear Mother, Liz is still the perfect wife AND the perfect mistress. She takes good care of me, and sometimes when we don't eat at the school she cooks yummy delicious meals. Not only that, but she has taught me the difficult art of appreciating good food. Not just enjoying a meal, but really tasting subtle flavors. It has been a long conspiracy of hers, but she is finally winning through."

He and Liz gained the love of the students. Mark Brady, a student at the school in Leysin, recalls that Royal--"who looked like an old man"--invited several of the young, athletic students to run up one of the nearby mountains. The students couldn't imagine that Royal would be able to keep up with them. They were surprised. "He was very fit," Mark remembers, "and was the first to the top." Mark recalls ski adventures Royal led the students on, how they explored new terrain, and how Royal's keen eye detected slopes that had possible avalanche danger. Royal would "shoot" the students one by one across these places. "He captured everyone's imagination, as well as respect."

156 Leysin students present Christmas presents to Royal and Liz

From Europe, Royal continued his duties as rock climbing editor with *Summit Magazine*. He and fellow ski-instructor Davy Agnew became co-performers in the production of a ski movie. Over Christmas, 1965, Royal and Liz borrowed a car and took a trip to Spain. He wrote in a letter: "In Spain one never eats supper before 9 p.m. and usually not before 10 p.m. ...and people are singing and yelling in the streets on their way home from dinner until 2:00. And then, to top this off, roosters start crowing in the middle of the city at 5 a.m.!!! Boy, did we have trouble getting rest."

During this time in Europe, Royal climbed with Yvon Chouinard on the colossal Dolomite walls of Italy. They managed the lofty North Face of the Cima Grande and other routes. Attempting an unclimbed wall on the Cima Ovest, they chopped forty-five bolts placed unnecessarily during attempts on the wall by European climbers. A huge overhang, however, turned Royal and Yvon back. They did not themselves want to start bolting.

157 Yvon Chouinard traverses in the Dolomites -- photo by Royal Robbins

Liz joined Royal for an ascent of one of the vertical classics in the Dolomites, the fifteen hundred-foot "Yellow Edge." This was one of the most thrilling and fun climbs she had ever done, and Royal and Chouinard later did a fast ascent of the route.

158 Looking down overhanging rock in the Dolomites
-- photo by Royal Robbins

At the suggestion of British writer-photographer John Cleare, the B.B.C. invited Royal to appear as "guest star" in a T.V. climbing "spectacular" to be transmitted live from the Anglesey sea cliffs of North Wales. Royal was to join legendary Joe Brown, along with Ian MacNaught Davis and Tom Patey. Patey--a Scottish climber, writer, and humorist--described this epic in his book *One Man's Mountains* as "The Greatest Show on Earth." Patey portrayed Royal in an essay as, "…outwardly serious and thoughtful, but with an occasional disarming smile that betrayed his keen sense of humor."

159 Royal Robbins instructs Tom Patey--wired for sound--how to use a carabiner. A bobby looks the other way -- photo by John Cleare

In the book *Mountains*, published in 1975 by Macmillan/London, John Cleare remembers of Royal: "He soon made an impression on the team of climbers assembled for the project; not just on the other stars, but the 'sherpas,' cameramen, and commentators alike. His rock climbing was delightful to watch and as superb as we had been led to believe. We soon discovered that his outwardly thoughtful and serious demeanor concealed wry stabs of humor.... My own particular memory of the programme was at the end, when Royal, belayed on the cliff top, was bringing Tom Patey up the final vertical wall. It had been aid climbing, and Royal had swung up through the overhangs with his usual effortless ease, while Tom, a brilliant ice climber, but not at home with 'mere gadgets,' was fighting and suffering every inch of the way. He finally emerged, rope draped and breathless on the cliff top. Royal looked hard at Tom's raw and bleeding hands. 'Back home in the States,' he remarked, 'they say you can always tell a good Aid-Man by his hands.' 'Lots of scars?' suggested Tom hopefully. Royal shook his head gently. 'No scars,' he said."

Later, in April of '66, Royal and Liz went together to England for a lecture and a climbing tour. Rock climbing here was, as Royal put it, "a man's sport." It was not a sexist remark so much as a keying in on a British colloquialism. Some very bold leads had been done by Joe Brown, Don Whillans, and others, without protection. Royal did a few 5.10 routes, including Brown's Left and Right Eliminates at Curbar, and with Frank Davis did Whillans' "fearful and brilliant Sloth."

The Right Eliminate involved a strenuous, sixty-foot, "gritstone" crack "not without risk." Sloth was also located on gritstone, approached by a short walk through heather, up a staircase of rock through a little forest. Its start involved ascending near-vertical rock with green moss and algae still wet from another day's drizzle. After perhaps fifty or sixty feet, a sling could be placed around a horn for protection, the only protection, for a huge overhang above. After a short glance outward at the distant slight hills of green, the several lakes, mist moving about in the rocks, and an acoustical clarity revealing every breath of damp, ancient, English air or scratch of climbing movement, Royal went out the underside of the large overhang with hands wedged in a crack.

In a letter I received from Royal, he wrote that these routes "were done years ago but required a full-scale effort by me." In *Summit Magazine*, he would write about Sloth, "My desire to do the climb overcame my fear of falling...." A fall from Sloth meant to drop free, out from under the overhang, like a bat.

161 Don Whillans -- photo by Ken Wilson

162 Joe Brown -- photo by Ken Wilson

In the Lake District of northern England, he climbed another short, fierce, overhanging crack, first done by Paul Ross, with the rather graphic name of "Bludgeon." In Wales, high on misty Llanberis Pass, Royal backed off Cenotaph Corner. He wanted to limit himself to only the scarce couple of points of protection used during the route's first ascent by Joe Brown. Royal had not hung from his fingers or exercised his climbing muscles for several months while skiing in Leysin and was not up to his usual strength. After a brief attempt, he invited his partner Joe Brown to lead the route. It was the second time Joe had climbed this distinctive inside corner since doing its first ascent. Royal watched and later wrote in an article that he had never witnessed such a display of mastery of rock climbing technique.

After following Brown up Cenotaph Corner, Royal soon returned in better shape and led the route with only Brown's original protection.

Royal also backed off of "Cemetery Gates," not wishing to pass yet through the veil. Far from his best shape, and unwilling to use a fixed piton that was added to the climb after its original natural ascent, he went down. In his climbing article later, he explained, "It is better to descend than engineer a climb that exceeds one's ability." As with Cenotaph Corner, he returned for another try of Cemetery Gates and succeeded, avoiding the fixed piton at the crux and honoring the style of the original ascent. Such a respecter of the spirit of truth, Royal found it necessary--essential--to do these climbs in a style in keeping with the philosophies of the area. He could have hammered pitons into Sloth to make it perfectly safe but did not wish to defile the bold, natural style employed by Whillans.

Royal was not only an instructor of climbing but was an instructor in the principles of truth. By brute honesty, he demanded these things of himself and, in so doing, communicated his esteem for other climbers.

The British had devised a technique of protection where common machine nuts threaded with a loop of sling were slotted downward into cracks. The rope running through a carabiner clipped to the sling afforded a point of protection. Royal quickly recognized that these methods were more creative, more adventurous and artful, and in some ways easier (they could be removed quickly and did not require carrying a hammer). They did not damage the rock, as did pitons.

163 Small nut wedged in crack -- photo by Harry Daley

"Nuts" would be another cause Royal would champion in America, and these efforts would revolutionize the American approach to the art of climbing. While a few people in America, including Chuck Pratt, would initially resist this movement toward nuts, it would soon become indisputable that nuts were the best answer to both preservation of the rock and refinement of the art. As always, Royal would set something to use--and after a measure of chaos in the climbing community, others would rush to make it theirs. As with hooks, big-wall haul techniques, and continuous ascents..., now ordinary machine nuts were soon to become the focus of the American climber's fascination.

Royal, Liz, and Tom Patey did the enjoyable "Agag's Groove" at Glencoe in a light rain. The rock was running with water. Their fingers were numb from the effort of clinging to small, cold holds on continuously steep face climbing. Royal would later write, "With those long, pitonless runouts, to err might be human, but it would also be fatal...."

Royal and Liz fell in love with the English and Scottish people. He recalls that he sang a little song he composed for a group of British climbers and earned their applause. It was, according to Royal, "a skilled effort toward versification. Note I was humble and didn't go so far as to call it poetry." The words of the song told of two passionate men: a certain Royal Robbins and a certain Warren Harding who had contrasting climbing philosophies....

From Britain, Royal and Liz went to Germany and, with money they borrowed from her parents, bought a Volkswagen Bus. They had been forced to sell their green Mercedes, after it was shipped to Europe. On their way through France, they visited the owner of Galibier Boots, "Monsieur Richard." Royal had been working as "technical advisor" in the designing of a shoe that would be suitable for Yosemite. Richard gave Royal and Liz a number of pairs of climbing shoes, including two pair each of the newly-designed, blue suede "R.R. Yosemite" (it would become known in America as the Robbins Boot). Royal recommended Chouinard as an American distributor for the boot.

Royal gave eighteen climbing lectures in the north of Spain in as many days, slides of El Cap and the Sentinel West Face film, translated by Jose Manuel Anglada, a good friend of Liz and Royal's who made the first Spanish ascent of the Eiger.

At one point, the bus was broken into. The thief foolishly stole three left feet of the climbing shoes!

Europe was, for Royal and Liz, a time of constant activity, imagination, and discovery. They climbed or skied almost every day. One can sense a little of the freedom, or excitement, from an excerpt of a letter Royal sent me dated June 20th, 1966: "We are now at a Chamonix hotel. As I look out the window, rain falls steadily. The Aguilles are hidden in mist. Two days ago a long dry spell was broken by a ferocious cold front that blasted in with little warning and the strongest winds I have seen in Europe, all accompanied by bolt after bolt of lightning." A sentence in an earlier part of that letter was Royal at his high-and-mighty best: "Your ability to think logically is improving, though I still occasionally spot a non sequitur."

Royal wrote the following letter on June 21, 1966:

"Dear Mother,

...We found the Spaniards extremely friendly, in general, and enjoyed ourselves.... We had our two cats with us, Ramases and her only surviving daughter, Littl'un.... On the way home, we stopped at a Mediterranean beach for lunch. Ramer disappeared, and hours of searching and calling were of no avail. We finally departed with Little'un, leaving Ramer to her fate. We asked a lady in the only house for miles to keep the cat with a green collar for us if she showed up. We returned to rainy Switzerland and after a couple of days met our American friend and ski client of mine, Jim, at Lausanne. He has come to Europe to climb the Matterhorn, and Liz and I will be with him for about a month, training, and finally guiding him up the peak of his dreams. He is paying all our expenses while we are together, and so we are living very well, staying in nice hotels, eating steak every night.... Also, Jim is generously buying us all we need in the way of climbing equipment. On the 6th of June we came to Chamonix from Lausanne to outfit Jim and us with climbing equipment. Then we departed for southern France to do some rock climbing in the Calanques, near Marseilles. On the way, we returned to where we had lost Ramases. And, miracle of miracles, we found our lost cat! She was a bit ragged and fearful after so many days in the sticks but was not much the worse for the wear. So then Royal, Lizard, Ramer, and Little'un continued their adventures with Jim. In the Calanques, we found out what a terrible fear of heights Jim has. It is going to be quite a challenge to me to overcome this sufficiently to get him up the Matterhorn. CAN WE DO IT? For the Answer, tune in next week to 'Alpine Circus' and follow the further adventures of Lizard, and Royal, and Ramer, and Littl'un...."

Jim kept Royal and Liz bursting with laughter--an "either laugh or cry" type of thing. With so much courage to dream and to try, however, there was no desire or reason to demean him. Royal felt that Jim's dream of climbing the Matterhorn far exceeded his abilities, but at least he dared to dream. Jim provided more than one unusual challenge for those whose care he was in, first in an unsuccessful bid to climb Mont Blanc and then on the Matterhorn. Liz recalls: "He had some real mental problems, including several serious phobias. He had acrophobia and fear of dead animals.... He was very adventurous and wanted to do great things, but his phobias would overcome him. On Mont Blanc, I was angry. We were almost to the top, but then he refused to go on. He sat down in the snow and wouldn't get up. On the Matterhorn, again, we were almost to the summit, and he wouldn't go any further. Several other climbing friends had joined in trying to help. We shielded him from the view down, but he ended up bringing the whole company down. Fear would send him to his knees. Royal would talk him back up onto his feet. He was a fine and generous person and would take us out to dinner. He wanted to sail, hired a crew and a boat but, I think, was afraid of water.... His desire for these adventures was an indication of his spirit, a spirit to which we were attracted."

In early September of '66, Royal arrived in Colorado with Liz and Don Whillans. I detected an air of competition between Whillans and Royal. Whillans, in particular, was somewhat standoffish toward Royal. He was not going to be viewed as another of Royal's talented foundlings. The three of us decided to do a somewhat low-key, six hundred-foot, 5.8 classic in Eldorado Canyon called Ruper. Whillans led up the crux crack with what might be called riotous speed, not clipping his rope to any of the fixed pitons. I was belaying, with Royal standing nearby on a ledge. As I noticed that the rope was running between Royal and the rock, I said to Royal, "If he falls, he'll pull you off."

"I'll take that chance," Royal replied.

164 Don Whillans (distant) and Pat Ament on Ruper, in Eldorado -- photo by Royal Robbins

Later in the afternoon, first Whillans and then Royal belayed me as I attempted the first lead of Supremacy Crack--a strenuous, 5.11 overhang in Eldorado. I had top-roped the first ascent of the crack a year earlier and now brought Royal and Don to it with the thought that they would demonstrate how it should be led. After a short try using nuts, Royal turned the lead over to me. He encouraged me to try to do the crack with nuts, but such an idea was too fantastic for me to give serious consideration at the time. The lead was made with pitons and a hammer, and with a few minor imperfections of style that produced a silent malcontent in Whillans. He scrambled down to take a nap by the river. I was vexed, as well as inspired, in the presence of these two arbiters of what was adequate.

When Royal followed the lead, he displayed his usual distinctive technique and, as he went up, hammered out the three pitons I had placed. Unable to overcome the combined strenuousness of the crack and having to hammer out the pitons, he was forced to rest--hanging for a short bit on one of the pitons.

They left for Yosemite where Whillans stepped up the competition. Royal wrote how on "the Crack Of Doom" Don found "a very Whillanesque solution"-- an ingenious but straightforward combination that enabled him to move up a section where Royal passed quite a bit of time and finally overcame only "by dint of brute force and determination." On Whillans' return to England by way of Colorado, he visited me and in so many words told me that he respected Royal-- with a few slight growls of reservation.

On their return to Europe in the fall, Royal and Liz visited Boulder again and gave a climbing lecture at the university. Two evenings later, racing in their Volkswagen Bus to stay just ahead of a snowstorm and then finding themselves overtaken by snow, sleet, rain, and ice, they arrived in Chicago where Royal gave another lecture. Then a program they were scheduled to give for the American Alpine Club in New York was a tighter fit than from Colorado to Chicago, requiring that they leave the Chicago lecture immediately (at midnight) and drive eight hundred and fifty miles in eighteen hours. They stayed in New York, with Jim McCarthy, and climbed in the Shawangunks, then flew to Luxembourg en route to Leysin.

Royal wrote in a letter: "December 11, 1966, Dear Mother, ...While we were waiting for our train, we had dinner in a restaurant at the station. I ordered a dish that I thought I was well acquainted with: 'Ris de veau,' which is (I thought) rice with a meat sauce made of veal and gravy. Unfortunately I didn't notice that the spelling of rice was different, instead of 'riz,' which means rice, it was 'ris,' which means sweet bread, more commonly known as, ugh, testicles! When I realized my mistake, my stomach turned, and I refused to continue eating. Luckily for me, true love came through, and Lizard traded me her hamburger steak for my plate of calf's BALLS! ....Right now it's full-fledged winter here (in Leysin), and...all the students (including 80 new ones who have heard how much fun it was last year) are very eager to ski and to do well...."

XI

Royal and Liz returned to America in April of '67. In May, they put up a classic free-climb in Yosemite they called "the Nutcracker Suite," where only nuts were used for protection. The route was five pitches in length (5.9 at its most difficult). Royal was making his point to the American climbing world that nuts were the way to go and that pitons were no longer fashionable (or possibly even ethical). Pratt, Chouinard, and Mort Hempel, in their own statement, put up a route nearby, using only pitons.

165 Royal "nutting" on Nutcracker Suite

From June 3rd to the 7th, 1967, Royal and TM Herbert spent just over four days on a new route on the West Face of El Capitan. In addition to the many pitons used in the ascent were fifty-seven sling runners and one hundred nuts. In two thousand feet of vertical rock, they had gotten away with only a single bolt. At one difficult place on the wall, a hook was placed with a two-foot length of stiff wire. Herbert recalls: "Royal got the hardest lead, up high in a corner. It was raining, and it was good that it worked out that way--because I wouldn't have been able to get up it. Fate always seems to have it that he gets the hard lead." It was imaginative climbing, by two masters. Later, on subsequent ascents, a number of bolts would be added by other climbing parties.

In the *Ascent Magazine* article recounting the route, Royal asked, "Is the hundredth bivouac different from the first?" He noted that he and TM "...were in a hurry. Fifty springs are indeed little room." Royal was beginning to feel the depth of experience behind him and the brevity of the experience ahead. He referred in the article to "the pitiful absurdity of the human condition." Absent a belief in God, the human condition perhaps could be viewed as pitifully absurd. In some sense, however, Royal's attitudes might easily have come from a believer. There was a kind of humility or reverence in being able to see the negligible and fleeting place man occupied. And as a spiritual seeker, he valued the ephemera and lessons, and the mystery, of mortality.

Also in June of '67, Royal and Chouinard were able to find fifteen sling runner placements and sixty-three nut placements in a two-day ascent of the North Wall of Grand Sentinel--in King's Canyon, south of Yosemite.

In July of '67, Royal and Liz climbed the Northwest Face of Half Dome in two and a half days. Liz's ability as a climber had risen over the years, and this was the first climb of a Grade VI by a woman. A few of her impressions from Half Dome: "You're way up there. It's thrilling and exposed. There's nothing to describe the beauty and exhilaration of being on that wall. The weather was hot, and I did the whole climb in cutoff jeans. Sleeping on a dinky ledge at night, I was amazed to find that it seemed commodious and comfortable. How could this be? Was I becoming a rugged outdoor woman? A chunk of salami, a sardine, a swallow of water were more enjoyable and satisfying up there than the grandest meal in a posh restaurant. I slept soundly."

166 Liz Robbins on the Northwest Face of Half Dome -- photo by Royal Robbins

167 Eyes as big as helmet (Liz on Half Dome) -- photo by Royal Robbins

On her traverse of the long, narrow, "Thank God Ledge" near the top of the wall, the steep rock above was trying to push her off. The ledge had looked easy from the start, but she ended in a crawl on one knee (the fashionable sophisticate). Her other leg dangled off the side of the ledge where two thousand feet of wall dropped below.

Throughout their life together, Liz was a tremendous source of support to Royal. As he had tried to sort out his identity, she remained a significant help to his self-belief. She was a pillar of strength, moving at will from a culture of refinement to a culture of adventure--and integrating the qualities of both.

She and he also attempted the Nose of El Capitan at this time but decided, after going up six hundred feet, that they were not prepared. They had brought too little water, etc.

168 Smile and frown, atop Half Dome
(Liz and Royal Robbins)

"NOW THE THIRD PITCH IS A FLARING
CHIMNEY WHICH ENDS IN A DIFFICULT
LIE-BACK! THEN — ..."

Style is the quality of the act of perception. For Royal, a new trip to the Canadian Rockies in the summer of 1967 brought some different angles on the phenomenon of elemental fate mixed with joy and vertigo. John Hudson, a six-foot-one, freckle-faced kid but strong mountaineer, pressed Royal's cardiovascular abilities in an ascent of the North Face of Mount Geikie.

170 Mt. Geikie -- photo by Royal Robbins

Slightly outmatched on the very athletic approach up steep terrain, Royal rationalized that he would make up the deficit on the rock. He wrote later, "We continually adjust our outlook to preserve our ego." At one place on Geikie, they climbed unroped up a steep rubble heap. It was delicate and dangerous. One error in judgment meant a fall of fifteen hundred feet. They spent the night on the top of the mountain in a seventy mile-an-hour west wind. The view was endless, the sky perfectly clear, the many Canadian peaks all around. It took twelve hours of the next day to make the difficult descent.

Royal wanted to learn mountaineering and, on an impulse, determined that the North Face of Mount Edith Cavell was a good place for his schooling. It was a lesson the magnitude of which was four thousand feet of rock, snow, and ice. Unable to find a climbing partner, he went by himself.

171 Mt. Edith Cavell -- photo by Royal Robbins

Unbelayed, high up the mountain on a slope of ice, he was "learning ice climbing fast." He realized that he should have belayed himself, but he "feared the time loss." It was dangerous, and he became immobilized at one point on the ice by his isolation and vulnerability. Should he go down? Yet it was so far down, and the top was so invitingly close. He felt that he would survive if he had the will and control to keep from making one hurried or panicky move.

On the summit rocks, hardly a hold could be trusted. He had to climb as though a fall didn't matter, but he knew it did. Four hours were spent on the upper six hundred feet. He climbed the final ten-foot snow wall unbelayed, discovering with horror--as he rolled onto the summit--that the snow wall might have given way and taken him with it. On the descent, a near fall--when he stepped too aggressively onto an ice slope--made him realize that "mountaineers aren't made in a day." Fred Beckey, a master alpinist and a devotee of the Canadian Rockies, told Royal afterward, "That was a pretty good stunt"--a compliment that meant something, because Beckey was, to Royal, not only a great climber but also a totally honest practitioner of his craft.

In autumn 1967, I raced out for a week or so to Yosemite and devoured hand cracks until they devoured the skin off the backs of my hands. Then I teamed with Royal and Dave Rearick one afternoon for an ascent of the Crack Of Doom. On the initial handjam of the route, I didn't like the pain of my torn hands against barbed rock and quickly gave the lead to Royal. He was in good form, always happy to better me. I led the long, scary, overhanging slot of the second pitch, and Royal complimented the lack of protection. He raced up the third rope-length, through a tight chimney similar to the Narrows on Sentinel. Rearick was out of shape for climbing, playing too much classical guitar and being a math professor, but fought onward and was enjoyable company.

The crux of the route, originally led in 1961 by Chuck Pratt, was now before us. Less steep and shorter than the three pitches below, it didn't look difficult at all. "Why don't you take this last, easy pitch," Royal said to me. He was not above sandbagging a friend for the pure entertainment of it. I led the pitch with only one mistake. I hammered a protection piton into a key finger hole. To move past the piton without the edge of a finger resting against the top of the piton was impossible. Royal made sure I knew I had touched the piton and that for all practical purposes I had used it. He wasn't going to let me get away with anything!

Royal once again had planned the ascent so that we would arrive atop the rock at dark, have to rappel in the night, and have to guess in large part as to whether or not the rappel anchors were good. In the talus forest, we applied great care weaving a trail downward through poison oak. With incredible precision, we stepped in and about what seemed in the darkness to be oak leaves. At the river at last, Royal relaxed and took off his shoes--only to get poison oak on his feet from a final bush hidden in the dark.

Royal, Liz, Rearick, Roper, Chouinard, the venerable Fritz Wiessner, and I enjoyed an ascent of Royal and Liz's classic Nutcracker Suite where we celebrated Fritz's birthday. He was well into his sixties and on the way to seventy, but with no sign of slowing at climbing. Fritz took us all to dinner afterward.

Without my asking him to do so, Royal recommended me to the American Alpine Club and gave me a personal endorsement for membership. I didn't see what was very important about being in the club, but it meant something to me to have his vote--or, as I deduced, his approval.

No sooner did this happen than we got into a brief spat. I wrote a letter to *Summit Magazine*, mentioning that I had, according to Pratt, authored the first

5.11 in Yosemite. I added that "one climber did... a number of difficult cracks in one week." I was referring to myself. Royal wrote a derisive, almost equally giddy, follow-up letter in the next issue of Summit.

172 Robbins camera-shy (a young Jim Bridwell looks on)
-- photo by TM Herbert

By way of foreword to these events, I had been impressed with a piece of Royal's writing, about his no-hands descent of Half Dome, where he modestly left out his own name: "Even one man went down without touching his hands." We all knew who that one man was. Trying to imitate Royal, I then wrote my, "One climber did..." and listed the host of difficult cracks I had done on my short trip out there. Royal's reply in Summit observed that by leaving off my name I was in fact trying to draw attention to myself. I answered him with a personal letter, reminding him of his own "modesty" in describing his no-hands descent, and he wrote me an apology.

In late winter of 1968, I happened to mention in a letter to Royal that I had been reading the Bible. He wrote back a terse farewell to me, stating, "We no longer have anything in common." I was ready at that time to give up God before I would give up my friendship with Royal. I wrote back to assure him that I hadn't joined a religion. I was only reading! He replied a few days later with a more amicable letter, rescinding the brusque goodbye.

XII

Royal and Liz were yearning for stability and a real profession. Their vagabond lifestyle had lost some of its attraction. Liz's hometown of Modesto, California, had become their home base, and her father offered Royal a job in the prospering family paint and wallpaper store (Valley Paint Company). The job was presented with an eye to Royal's one day taking over the business.

They moved into their own house and began to feel very "homey."

When I went to Yosemite in spring of '68, Royal was there too and was attempting to climb El Capitan alone! He was hoping to make the first solo ascent of those three thousand-feet. The ascent was into about its eighth day, and Liz and I stood out in El Cap meadow in April light to try to see him. Even through a small pair of opera glasses that Liz had, Royal was a red dot about the size of the head of a pin. At one point, while looking upward through the glasses, Liz offered the quirky, "Good move, Royal."

The Muir Wall, Royal's choice for a route, was first done by TM Herbert and Chouinard. It was about the only thing on El Cap Royal hadn't done, and the route did not yet have a second ascent. It was Royal's biggest rock climbing undertaking and was potentially the most dangerous. He admitted later in an article that the climb was not perfectly in hand at every turn. Wind whipped him with "chilling fury."

A question went through his soul: "Will those who search for peace through achievement ever be satisfied?" Indeed, time was moving away with him. Where was he going? What did he have to look forward to as a climber? A new generation of climbers--including Jim Madsen and Kim Schmitz--was establishing itself and making the fastest ascents yet of big-walls. As Royal later wrote in *Summit Magazine*: "Royal Robbins, attempting to prove he's not as old as he is...succeeded in proving...he's a heavy when it comes to patience."

He spent nights tied to pitons, suspended in his hammock. He reflected about the adventures of great alpinists, such as the Italian, Walter Bonatti. Royal felt that Bonatti's solo achievements were not technological tricks but were primarily achievements of the human spirit.

73 El Capitan -- photo by Tom Frost

It was clear, through Royal's several later writings about his solo of El Cap, that there was a lot of self-examination with regard to his motives. He was like the poet Yeats, who said once in a talk that "Every motive must be followed, through all the obscure mystery of its logic." Royal wondered if to solo El Cap was a way of showing off. He felt that it was a way of exploring himself. "One is looking at oneself all the way up," he reflected. "But will the spirit be stronger afterwards?"

The route required that he climb a section of rock, then rappel back, then jumar up that same section of rock to remove the gear. In essence, the three thousand feet had to be covered three times. He began to hate these repetitions and hated the tedium. The head of his hammer broke off suddenly from too much use, but fortunately he had a spare in the haul bag. If the second hammer broke, a rescue would be necessary. No one yet had tried to send a cable down from the top or perform a major rescue on El Cap.

On the first day of the climb, when he was a pitch or so above the ground, his rope had gotten stuck below him. Dick McCracken--a friendly face from the past, who was in Yosemite working on a film with Glen Denny, Lito Tejada-Flores, and Gary Colliver--materialized like a guardian angel out of the oak trees and scrambled up to free the rope.

At one point high on the wall, when far above his protection and risking a dangerous, self-belayed fall, Royal felt a subtle panic--something dangerous, something insidious--and was forced to slow up and think about things, a very smart move. He realized that he needed to bring himself back into control of the situation.

It was a lonely place to be, with only his thoughts for conversation, or his grumblings, or the wind. When the seventh day was clear and beautiful, he "praised the lord."

Three hundred feet from the top, he encountered a section of rock that was marginally climbable by the first ascent team and now was going to mean great risk as a solo self-belay. At an extremely difficult section, he used a RURP and after an effort fitted a tiny nut. The nut held his weight at first, but then the rock around it crumbled. He fell, and the RURP held his fall. He decided that the danger was too great at this spot, and he was forced to do something he had never yet done in his career: drill a bolt on an already existing route. From the point of view of his own rigorous ethic, this meant, in a sense, defeat.

His final night on the wall was spent hanging on sheer rock in a hammock.

174 Royal Robbins approaches the summit of the Muir Wall of El Capitan
-- photo by Glen Denny

175 Steep rock near the top of the Muir Wall of El Cap
-- photo by Glen Denny

176 Royal reaches the top of El Capitan, solo -- photo by Glen Denny

The ascent required nine and a half days, and he was greeted at the top the final morning by Glen Denny, other friends, and by the love of his life: Liz.

Denny recalls: "It was a warm, sunny day. It struck me that Royal kept his sweater on. His bodily system was possibly winding down, showing strain. He wasn't putting out the heat he normally would have."

Peter Viereck wrote, "...magic that believes itself must die." There was doubt, precious, significant, vital doubt as to what Royal had achieved or could achieve in climbing.

177 Royal and Liz Robbins, summit of El Capitan
-- photo by Glen Denny

Royal wrote to his mother on the 13th of June, 1968: "Dear Mom, ...I have even, believe it or not, taken to working in the garden! Not too much of course. After all, I have other interests, but enough to help appearances and to get some exercise. It's a really healthful thing to do. You get exercise for the body and at the same time provide food for the soul (and also food for the belly, for Lizard is raising tomatoes, cucumbers, and sumpin or udder). Anyway, it's kind of fun, and there's even a chance I might begin to take pride in my home and garden! That reminds me--I must buy a hoe today, to get those damn weeds!"

In late June, Royal climbed with me on the beautiful, knobby domes of Tuolumne.

179 Royal Robbins and Pat Ament in Tuolumne -- photo by Steve Roper

Later we were joined by Tom Higgins. The unfiltered, high-country sun burned our skin. Tom and I were caught up in the jocose spirit that we had long come to associate with Tuolumne climbing. Royal seemed tired from his nine and a half days on El Cap and, on belay ledges, gazed off into space. After so many days alone on the Muir Wall, he did not seem to know what to do with conversation. Yet he competed with us, as though he were a young man at Tahquitz Rock attempting to live up to a burden of renown.

180 Royal twirls nut on finger (Liz and Royal Robbins in Tuolumne)
-- photo by Pat Ament

Royal had left his mark everywhere from the Shawangunks of New York to crags in Illinois to the lesser known Buttermilks near Bishop on the east side of the Sierra. Everywhere, he had led or pioneered a test piece. And everywhere, there existed a person who could boast of a personal climb that Royal had struggled at or failed on. To be a great climber meant to have ambitious, young competitors try to bring you down into the arena of their own understanding. Yet Royal was getting a sense of the game, growing less troubled by his critics and more desirous that he validate genuinely good climbers by doing and appreciating routes that were theirs. He acknowledged the inspiration that he drew from the achievements of others.

Royal was more often able to see himself in a lighter spirit. In a 1969 *Scottish Mountaineering Club Journal*, describing a certain Scottish climber, Royal would write, "He...proceeded to win the respect of the hypercritical, snobbish Yosemite climbers."

John Gill, the one person who could have vaunted his achievements, with so many instances where he was able to outdo all other climbers, was a supreme example of modesty. He stated openly that he felt Royal was a greater climber than himself--and a "real" climber, by virtue of his tremendous big-wall achievements.

Royal and old friend Joe Fitschen made a three-day ascent of the South Face of Mount Watkins in Yosemite in June of '68. When they got down off the wall, Fitschen found that he was offered a teaching job in Susanville, California. What this meant was that he could climb the rest of the summer without financial worry, and Royal was an eager accomplice. They stormed the Yosemite rock and also went to the Cascades in Washington where they did a climb. This was en route to a five-day climbing clinic Royal gave in British Columbia. While in Canada, they thought to attempt Sherrick's route on Mount Robson, but the weather was completely socked in.

XIII

Paint was not the solution for Royal Robbins. After nine months, he quit the store, "almost unconsciously," and rededicated himself to climbing. He stated later in a *Summit Magazine* interview, "I just had the faith that if I devoted myself to what I loved, then everything else would take care of itself." He used the word "faith" a lot, but it was synonymous with self-belief. When Layton Kor went through a religious conversion, Royal regarded it as a mild sort of defection from the elite circle of climbers--the independent, footloose nonbelievers.

In their spare time, Royal and Liz had begun importing and marketing Galibier rock and mountain boots. They shipped them from their garage. The kitchen became an office, and the dining room table became a desk. At dinner time, the typewriter and files were swept from the table and the room transformed anew into domesticity. It was cause for slight consternation now that they had given the distributorship of their own "Robbins boot" to Chouinard. It made sense to try to get it back. They struck a deal with Chouinard and Frost, an offer that Royal and Liz almost had to refuse--but didn't.

Chouinard's entrepreneurial "ruthlessness" did not put Royal off and, for Royal, indicated Yvon's strong focus toward his ends.

Late October of '68, a snowstorm trapped Warren Harding and Galen Rowell halfway up the South Face of Half Dome. They were attempting the first ascent of this wall. Harding had been through many trials by fire in summer heat in Yosemite, including his first ascent of El Capitan, but now was in a trial of ice. The rain and snow were minor compared to a torrent that ran into and out of a shallow recess in which the climbers had situated themselves. Water filled the hammock-tents in which they were hanging, and the two climbers became thoroughly drenched, their ropes frozen. Fearing that they might not survive another night, they made a transmission with a small walkie-talkie. Just before the walkie-talkie died, they asked if a rope could somehow be dropped to them from above.

A number of climbers were summoned to the scene, including Royal who drove up from Modesto, and were transported by helicopter to the snowy crown of Half Dome. They carefully uncoiled a twelve hundred-foot length of goldline and laid it out in long strips like fire hose, ready for the descent. A couple of 3/8-inch bolts were drilled for anchors. As a second rope, they tied together five one hundred and fifty-foot perlon ropes.

It was below freezing, but a full moon lit the scene brilliantly. Tied to the goldline and the perlon, Royal was lowered hundreds of feet down the face to where he was able to deliver fresh down jackets, gloves, and hot soup to the suffering climbers.

The rescue ropes became icy and difficult to ascend, and Harding's down-pants were frozen, but the two climbers were able to prusik to the top where tents were pitched and everyone spent the night. Where differing philosophies had tended to foster enmities, now Royal was a peer who had come to the aid of fellow climbers. Royal took in the magnificent, starlit view from the summit of Half Dome. Across the valley was the dark silhouette of Mount Watkins' South Face where Harding four years earlier had participated in a bold, continuous first ascent with Pratt and Chouinard. Although Royal differed with some of Harding's principles, he liked Harding and respected him as an individual.

181 Helicopter, summit of Half Dome, morning after rescue
-- photo by Royal Robbins

In 1968, Royal and Liz began their own climbing school, Rockcraft, often meeting with students during the spring or summer months at the rocks of Lover's Leap near Lake Tahoe. Liz recalls, "It was a lot of fun and a lot of work. It was funny, one challenge and adventure and fiasco after another, taking people around to different areas...." Royal liked this involvement with people, the process of outward-reaching, and was a master at helping neophytes discover the joys of how a technique worked. For a number of years to come, he would give of his experience to students, and receive of their joy, an exchange worth more than the fee for the classes. He was looking beyond his own goals, to the goals of other people.

Yet being a climbing instructor did not mean that he was over the hill and relegated to the role of teacher. He was still fit and free-climbing ferocious Yosemite cracks, and making first ascents of a number of these, such as the painful, skin-trashing "Meat Grinder" and "Vendetta."

During this time, Royal seemed, through my eyes, to take a few weird steps "sideways" along "the progression." One night at their Modesto home, I found him to be exasperating--not quite sinister, but cynical. After dinner, I was invited to show slides of an ascent I had made of El Cap. As I identified ledges and features of the climb, Royal repeated my comments to Liz and chuckled with her--as though they didn't have to be told what the features of the climb were. It felt as though--if it were possible--he would freak me out or that, if he could, he would hand me a firecracker cigar and wait with a smile for me to light up. I gazed away into a drawing of Don Quixote that hung in a picture frame on a wall.

At a late hour, when Royal had finished with me, he turned to their cat. With the cat lying on its back, Royal spun it on the slippery tile floor of a hall until the cat was so dizzy it could barely walk. Then Royal rolled a tiny ball down the hall. A somber atmosphere turned to hysteria as the cat bounced back and forth off the walls of the hallway, attempting to run after the ball. It was a game that the cat loved. It returned for another spin.

The Robbins Boots were selling in '69, and Royal and Liz were importing and marketing other Galibier mountain boots and rock climbing shoes. They dubbed their company "Mountain Paraphernalia."

In the later '60s, Royal and Liz rode a freight train to Portland, Oregon, with Steve Roper, for an American Alpine Club meeting. Royal of course had hopped a lot of freights as a kid, and Roper had been doing it as an adult and was savvy as to freight train schedules. They set off, knowing that it was going to be cold and miserable and bumpy but wonderful. They shipped their dress clothing ahead. On the train, in a storm, they hung a tarp to create a tent. Wet, tired, and dirty, they walked from the Portland train yard and called a taxi. Looking like tramps, they arrived at the elegant hotel where they were pre-booked and where the meeting was being held.

Royal and Liz spent Christmas in England in 1969 with Bev Clark and his wife and family and then visited Leysin again, and met up with old friends such as Mick Burke, in the process of helping Bev make a poetic ski film.

June 1969, Royal and artist-photographer Glen Denny made the first ascent of the tall, sleek Prow on the East Face of Washington Column. Yosemite still had big walls and, in this case, minor big walls to be climbed. The route was complicated and was climbed creatively.

First ascents of Mount Nevermore, Mount Jeffers, and Mount Sasquatch, in the solitude of the remote Cathedral Spires of Alaska with Joe Fitschen and Charlie Raymond from early July to the first of August of '69 added three major alpine walls to Royal's story. After a drive of thirty-five hundred miles (including eleven-hundred miles of gravel road), the climbers were flown into the Cathedral Spires area by the ace bush-pilot of Alaska, Don Sheldon, who landed on a glacier. Each of the cold, snow-covered, sweeping granite walls that they climbed was two to three thousand feet in height and involved precarious ridges, ice caves, crevasses, difficult route-finding up huge distances of rock, and endless rappels to descend. Rain and winds added challenge to the climbing-- mixed rock and ice, with very difficult chimneys, cracks, traverses, and aid-climbing, chilled by mist and storms but kept warm by the strength of friendship.

182 Joe Fitschen, Alaska -- photo by Royal Robbins

183 Charlie Raymond, Alaska -- photo by Royal Robbins

XIV

From September 30th to October 7th, 1969, Royal and Don Peterson--a young volcano (he was given to eruptions)--placed themselves under each other's influence for the length of time necessary to ascend the two thousand-foot, blank, black-streaked center of the Northwest Face of Half Dome.

The dreaded summit overhangs were the unavoidable conclusion of this climb, and smooth, crackless sections of rock would demand shrewd, calculating aid-work to keep this first ascent from becoming a bolting debacle.

84 Half Dome -- photo by Tom Frost

A year earlier, Royal had made an attempt on the route with Pratt and Dennis Hennek. Realizing that they had brought too few bolts and were low on water, they retreated. When it was time for the next try at the route, Hennek was suffering from an injury while Pratt had misgivings--something about Royal's intensity interfering with the right spirit of the climb. Royal recruited the nearest able body: the young, cocksure Peterson.

Royal named the route "Tis-sa-ack," after a mythical Indian woman whose tears fell and created the wide black streaks down the wall.

On this route the forces of respectability were put to rout, and Royal--in addition to some brilliant aid-climbing--had to spend long, agonizing hours drilling bolts. It was a violation of his own hatred of bolting. A bolt-ladder established during the attempt with Pratt and Hennek was one of the most craftsmanlike bolt ladders anywhere. The bolts were driven well and placed far apart. High on the wall, however, in the company of Peterson, drills broke, bolts went in poorly, and the necessity that they hurry decreed that some of the bolts be placed only part way in. Other bolts had to be removed for use higher. Royal admitted that this was, unfortunately, some of the poorest bolting anywhere.

185 Royal leading on Tis-sa-ack -- photo by Don Peterson

Royal had to marshal his years of experience and move out far along the thin edge of safety in order to climb a rock face of this infinite smoothness and stature. Cracks five inches wide--too wide for pitons and too narrow to fit the body inside--required desperate free-climbing that even the aggressive, impatient Peterson was happy to let Royal lead. A hook placed beyond their reach, by lifting it up on the wire of a nut, saved a bolt.

186 Telephoto of Tis-sa-ack, Robbins and Peterson   -- by Glen Denny

On the summit overhangs, the piton Royal was hanging from pulled out just as he clipped to the next piton higher. Then a piton below fell out, by itself, with no weight on it. In darkness, Royal finished the last of the climbing--feeling for cracks with his fingers, hitting his fingers with his hammer, and pitons pulling out.... He stood again at the top of Half Dome.

Glen Denny had gone up via the cable route and was on the summit waiting. They all spent the night there. Denny recalls, "Peterson and Royal were hostile toward each other. In the morning, Peterson really didn't want to be in the photo Royal asked me to take of them."

Almost more of a triumph than this climb of Tis-sa-ack was the brilliant article that Royal wrote about it in *Ascent Magazine*. He jumped to a higher level of creativity as a writer. One theme of the article was the tendency of the climbers to destroy each other's confidence, in their clash of temperaments. The remarkable feature of the writing was how Royal presented the first-person thoughts of both climbers. In other words, he wrote Peterson's thoughts! For example, Peterson (actually Royal): "What I didn't like was his assumption of superiority. Like he figured just because he was Royal Robbins he was the leader.... When we got up to the base of the wall he sent me to fetch water." Pretending to know Peterson's thoughts allowed Royal to scrutinize himself, to observe (and face) aspects of his own life which were legendary and with which he was not altogether comfortable. The writing was also a way for Royal to play. He portrayed his own silent intimidation, the confounding sides of himself, along with his despair at the endless-seeming wall above and the ecstatic character of being in a place so contrary.

Royal wondered in one sense if he were marking time in a prolonged adolescence. Or were these climbs a rational, sustained program of action toward a goal? Did the tasks of overcoming huge rock faces actually bring growth? There was a faint distinction between a short-lived fulfillment by fantasy and having initiative toward a clear, positive maturity or vision. Moved once by that rash, imaginative power of being young, he was now governed by a purgative process--tangled in part with contempts within himself.

Part of the "purification" demanded that a person arrive at what he or she was capable of being, that there be a strengthening, sometimes passing through the center of fear, danger, and doubt. Royal was a climber in the spirit of the poet Keats: "...certain of nothing but the holiness of the Heart's affections and the truth of Imagination." Younger, it was power exercised in excess of understanding. Now it was the memory of a multitude of previous images that seemed to loom onward, one big wall that led to the next.

The business was expanded in 1970 to include rock climbing gear, and they opened a retail climbing shop in Modesto.

On May 26th and 27th of '70, as though there were still much more to do, Royal soloed a new route up the fourteen hundred-foot right side of the West Face of Sentinel Rock. In *Summit Magazine*, he offered a modest amount of information about the route, one highlight being an unprotected jam-crack that left him "a little shaky." One could intuit something from the route's name, "In Cold Blood." A description in Steve Roper's guide to Yosemite spoke of difficult aid-climbing (A4), pendulums, RURPS, and lassoing a flake.... In Royal's article about the climb, he rebuked Curtis Casewit, a "renowned authority on mountaineering," for saying, "Solo climbing is insanity."

Royal was also quite vocal about the continuing use of pitons. In *Summit Magazine*, July-August 1970, he wrote: "The Higher Spire is now more difficult because a critical flake has been knocked off by the injudicious and unnecessary placement of a piton behind it. The routes on Ranger Rock, like many moderate and accessible climbs in this country, are dying from piton erosion...repeated placement and removal of pitons. The destruction on one of these routes, the Nutcracker, is especially severe, and especially painful as this climb is susceptible to safe ascent solely with artificial chockstones (nuts)."

In July of '70, in four days of climbing, Royal devised yet another route up the North Wall of Half Dome, a route done with Dick Dorworth that they named Arcturus. Their worst adversary was rockfall from hikers tossing granite from the summit, and there were dangerous loose blocks on the wall on the upper part of the climb. Another problem was heat. Royal ate very little during the climb and felt better only after they made it to the top.

Then in October, as a guide, Royal repeated his new route on the West Face of Sentinel with an anesthesiologist and wife--Egon and Johanna Marte. Climbs once viewed as extremely formidable were becoming relaxed holidays for professionals!

Somewhere during this period, Royal, Chuck Pratt, and Steve Roper climbed together in Utah and made an ascent of the Titan--Layton Kor's very tall, red, mud-coated, desert tower rising out of Castle Valley. In the book *Canyon Country Climbs*, by Katy Cassidy and Earl Wiggins, Roper wrote of this ascent and expressed resentment about being thrust into a subservient role by "the Master." Roper referred to himself as "a sheep," or that he felt so when Royal took charge of setting the rappel anchors. The climbers returned from the ascent, covered in dried mud and red rock-dust.

Just when everyone thought Harding was in control of his bolting, he and Dean Caldwell made the first ascent of "the Wall of the Early Morning Light" on El Capitan, in November of '70. Three hundred and thirty-three holes were drilled into the rock--holes for bolts and for rivets and for hooks. Harding and Caldwell had lasted an unbelievable number of days on the wall--almost a month. Quite an amount of publicity that seemed to have been rigged beforehand added to the resentment that other climbers felt, including Robbins. Harding had helped to invent Yosemite climbing but also was participating in its degradation--what Royal called "the idle drilling of holes in rock just to get up."

El Capitan was, to Royal, a wide, beautiful canvas upon which to paint adventures, substantial, not cheap.

In late January of '71, in the middle of winter, Royal and Don Lauria started up the route with a cold chisel and the intent of removing the bolts and the route. If such routes were allowed, a future route, after all, might use six hundred bolts. If there was to be a distinction between what was acceptable and what was not acceptable, this was the time to make it. But after Royal had removed forty of the bolts, he began to have second thoughts. He was beginning to appreciate the difficulty of the climbing, despite its many bolts. The non-bolted sections of the route were strenuous. He recognized Harding's faults but also acknowledged Harding's toughness and counted him as one of his friends. Harding was, in Royal's words, a "satirical rogue" with "slashing verbal attacks" who "enjoyed an image of drunkenness," yet who also was genuine and defined his own reality.

Hanging on the wall, awake in his hammock, Royal began to seriously think about what he was doing. He decided that he no longer felt right about destroying the route. His inner feelings were not going along with it. Who was he to tell others how to climb? He began to realize that he should have kept his opinions at the statement level and not on the enforcement level. Anyway, removing mass bolts was nearly as crass as putting them in. He felt as though he were hitting Harding with every blow of the hammer. Royal's humility got the best of him. Yet he and Lauria continued up the route and, on February 4th of '71, after six days of climbing, reached the top.

For the first time, Harding spoke out and announced to the climbing world that he did not answer to Royal Robbins. Climbing was an expression of individuality, as Harding saw it, and he was angry with those who would set themselves up as "ethical spokesmen." Harding requested the right to place bolts as he pleased.

Royal's bolt removals reinforced the antagonism felt toward him by rivals. It was a famous, unpleasant chapter of Yosemite climbing for both Harding and Royal, and one person was likely as damaged as the other. Yet it was a milestone that no one would soon have to go through again, because the point seemed to "take" with the climbing community. For some time, climbers would lean toward Royal's view. They were adequately repulsed by the over-bolting of big walls. And Royal was, with this affair, slowly becoming more separated from Yosemite and from his guardianship of the celestial Eden that had afforded so much happiness in golden days.

187 Looking west, through Yosemite Valley -- photo by Tom Frost

XV

In 1971, La Siesta Press published Royal's *Basic Rockcraft*--a modest book of climbing instruction that carried on in the tradition of past great teachers of climbing. The book's success in selling more than two hundred thousand copies was a tribute to the strength of the information but also to the admiration felt for Royal by the climbing populace. He seemed to incorporate the adventurer with the stylist, the careful planner, the forward thinker, and philosopher. He had come away from the Wall of the Early Morning Light bruised but possibly the victor in the battle. A number of big-wall climbers--Billy Westbay, Kim Schmitz, Dennis Henneck, Don Lauria, Chuck Kroger, and others, and perhaps the greatest of these, Charlie Porter--were beginning to carry on in Royal's imposing, adventurous style.

188 Charlie Porter

Jim Bridwell, an especially talented Yosemite crack climber in the spirit of Pratt and Sacherer, was also a big-wall climber who earned Royal's respect. Bridwell recalls that Royal humbled himself one day to seek his advice on the techniques required to climb Pratt's bold off-width, "the Twilight Zone."

189 Jim Bridwell -- photo by Ken Wilson

In the early '70s, Royal made a significant attempt to solo a new route on the vertical and overhanging, eighteen hundred-foot wall between the North America Wall and the East Buttress of El Cap. Royal comments on this attempt:

"I had done some really hard climbing. I'd saved six or seven bolts by throwing nuts above, into cracks. Not quite half way up the wall, after three days of climbing, I ran out of steam. I didn't have enough fight. It was not a climb

I'm proud of. I didn't push myself. I let myself get overwhelmed by it. I took the easy way out. On the fourth day, I came down."

Liz and Royal's first child, Tamara, was born in September of 1971.

In the winter of '71, Royal left with Yvon Chouinard and Doug Tompkins on a three-week climbing expedition to South America. It was summer in Patagonia. Royal and Chouinard had notions of an attempt of the huge Cerro Torre, but the weather was bad and never did break. They were unable to get up anything. The height of the trip was to fly around Cerro Torre in Doug's small plane, the wind blowing "around two hundred miles an hour."

190 Chouinard in Patagonia
-- photo by Royal Robbins

This turned out to be a difficult time for Liz, left with the sole care of a newborn. Royal was not certain yet if he could ever make a serious commitment as a father. Liz wondered, during the three weeks that he was away, if she was having their child alone. Royal regretted leaving them for that period of time. To Royal, looking back on this, it seemed monstrous to have left his wife and newborn daughter, but such was the strength of the climbing imperative within him. At the time, he hardly gave leaving a second thought. He had to climb.

" 'CERTAINLY GETS LONESOME OUT
ON THESE BIVOUACS , DOESN'T IT ?."

Some of Royal's friends lost track of him during the early '70s, although he did not lose track of himself. He and Liz opened another climbing equipment store in 1971 in Fresno, California. He raced up the Salathe-Steck on Sentinel in ten hours with Doug Scott and Tony Wilmott. He was climbing in Tretorn tennis shoes which he felt were the best combination of comfort and rock climbing performance. These were not the usual stiff climbing shoes that provided support on small holds. They could not be jammed into cracks the way the hard Robbins Boot could. Yet Royal was climbing better than ever. In his Tretorn tennis shoes, he climbed the Salathe Wall of El Capitan with a friend from Madison, Wisconsin. He climbed the Direct North Buttress of Middle Cathedral Rock in Tretorns and also led his friends Egon and Johanna Marte up the Salathe Wall of El Capitan. El Cap now was hosting guided tours.

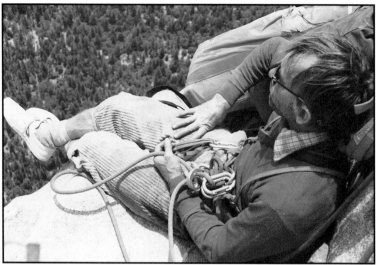

192 Royal spaces out on a ledge on the Salathe Wall of El Capitan (note Tretorn tennis shoes)

In late April 1972, Liz and Royal left Tamara in the care of friends and took a journey down the Green River by raft. They spent three weeks on the Green, starting at Flaming Gorge Dam in Utah and traveling two hundred and ninety miles, the first of many rivers they would run together. Rivers were to become another way of finding adventure in beautiful, natural settings.

In 1973, La Siesta Press published Royal's second book: *Advanced Rockcraft*.

Kayaks were added to the wares of Mountain Paraphernalia, and Royal thought that it would be a good idea to learn this form of river running. Bill Yard, a Modesto kayaker, taught him how to master white water.

One day at the base of El Cap, in May 1974 on the shorter pinnacle routes, Royal solo free-climbed "Ahab" (a 5.10 off-width originally led by Frank Sacherer). From the top of Ahab, he downclimbed "Moby Dick," all in his Tretorn tennis shoes. He free-soloed the exacting 5.11 start to "the Slack," continued up the Slack, crawled through the space behind the pinnacle, and climbed down the strenuous lower pitches of the left side of the Slack.

193 Royal Robbins recharges his batteries on Limey ale, Highgate, London, 1973 -- photo by John Cleare

194 El Cap -- photo by Pat Ament

Elsewhere in Yosemite during the early and mid-'70s, Royal free-soloed the difficult off-width cracks that form the Right and Left sides of Reed Pinnacle (both 5.10). These illustrations of mastery were daring enough with a rope and in regular climbing shoes, much less free-solo and in his Swedish-made, low-cut, flimsy tennis shoes. This was, arguably, the highest standard of free-solo climbing in the world at the time. He also free-soloed the left side of the Cookie (5.10), Chingando (5.10), Moby Dick-Left Side (5.10-), the Crack of Despair (5.10 off-width), and the East Buttress of El Capitan (5.10). He made countless other solo ascents of slightly less difficulty (such as Commitment, 5.9, Cleft, 5.9, the Mouth, 5.9, and the Right and Center routes on the Cookie, both 5.9). Several of these routes were conservatively graded and closer to 5.10 than 5.9. Royal self-belay soloed many longer routes, including the North and Direct North Buttresses of Middle Cathedral Rock.

The climbing was now an affirmation, rather than an outgrowth of questions within himself.

In this year, something simple but important occurred that foreshadowed an impending and major change in the direction of their business: the addition of sweaters to their mountaineering line.

In the May 1975 *Mountain Gazette*, Royal returned to his thoughts of Warren Harding and further repented the deed of erasing Harding's bolts. Royal wrote, "Such bolt chopping is merely a way of underlining one's own superiority and shows ruthless contempt for the work of other men." Royal added, "I, for one, have had a bellyful of those exquisite moralists who complain constantly about minor human vices." Royal celebrated Harding's audacity and Harding's authenticity.

Royal did not, however, celebrate a book called *Climbing In North America*, authored by English climber Chris Jones and published by the American Alpine Club in conjunction with the University of California Press. This was a beautifully published book, profusely decorated with memorable historical photos, but with a surprisingly superficial, sometimes erroneous text. Royal felt demeaned (as did other people) by fabrications, rumor, exaggerations, and stories that were largely the product of rivals or hearsay. Royal speculated that perhaps Jones needed to malign people in order to feel a sense of authority over his subjects. That Royal was described as "an intense, humorless competitor" was not something Royal contested. There were enough people who had gotten such an impression, due to Royal's quiet way, and Royal could not fault mere opinion. But other depictions within the book were ridiculous, such as an account of Royal in the Tetons in the 1960's disdaining to engage in a pushup contest with the Vulgarians--a group of New York climbers who worked hard to deserve their name and who became notorious for actions away from the climb rather than on. Royal supposedly went off to a secret place in the forest of Jenny Lake Campground to hide and practice pushups. Someone then spied Royal doing his pushups in that private place in the forest. Later, according to the tale, Royal appeared upon the scene and offered the same challenge of a pushup contest to the Vulgarians.

Royal noted that this apocryphal story was out of character and that he was such an intense competitor that he wouldn't have hesitated to be part of such a contest win or lose. And why would he sneakily practice pushups anymore than he would secretly practice boulder problems? The answer was that he wouldn't, because his own opinion of himself was always far more important than what others thought. He felt that if Jones had cited his real faults, which were adequately numerous, he would have pled guilty, but some of the examples cited simply never happened. Perhaps these were merely Jones' imperfect handling of the fanciful lore that seemed to generate around Royal, rather than a statement that Jones was anti-Robbins, but Royal felt that it was to the discredit of the American Alpine Club and the University of California Press to have these misrepresentations in a book so potentially important. He decided not to say anything at the time but made a mental note to one day set the record straight.

Royal was made an honorary member of the Alpine Club less than a year after the book's publication. He wondered if "they" were in some way trying to make it up to him.

I gave a climbing slide-show at Royal's mountaineering shop in Modesto in about spring of '75. Royal didn't make the slide show, because he and Liz were at the ballet in San Francisco. The morning after the show, I got to meet Tamara. Although only about six years old, she corrected me on something I said and did so with the same contentiousness that might have been employed by Royal. He chuckled, "That-a girl, you tell 'em."

Around the summer of 1976, Liz was kayaking and had a close call where she capsized in the Mokelumne River in the Sierra Nevada. She was washed through low-hanging trees and branches but survived.

Soon after this, she and Royal passed through Colorado briefly. Royal and I did a hurried ascent of Eldorado's "T-2" route, and I was impressed with how strong he was. He had no trouble at any point on the six hundred-foot route, including the muscle-taxing overhang at the start. The next day, the Eldorado wind was too frigid for me to want to climb, even with Royal. We roped up at the base of the West Buttress of the Bastille. I shivered and looked around. Royal got the picture, we unroped, and he let me walk about in the bottom of the canyon as he soloed to the highest point of Redgarden Wall.

A day or so later, as though for nostalgia's sake, we decided to try our 1964 "Athlete's Feat." I rubbed my fingers with gymnastic chalk--a tool John Gill had introduced to bouldering and to climbing in the Tetons in the 1950's, and that I had introduced into Eldorado and Yosemite in the '60s, and which Royal still had reservations about. The first moves of Athlete's Feat were by no means easy for him this time, even with a top-rope. Liz watched from below. After he tried a couple of times, she offered the sarcastic, "You'd better chalk up, Royal, you can't do it without chalk." Royal didn't answer, but smiled. He was looking at climbing, wondering perhaps how he might pick up those lost parts of himself and make them alive again.

I had visions during these years of writing a biography of Royal. When I asked him if he would consider my doing so, he said that he was going to write it himself.

195 In Langdale, in the Lake District of England, September 1976, with Tamara -- photo by John Cleare

Promiscuous in his love of experience, Royal stole away in August of '76 for another Alaskan adventure where he and Joe Coats managed to accomplish a large peak in the Cathedral (Kitchatna) Spires.

Liz and Royal visited the gorgeous, alpine setting of Telluride, Colorado, lured by the invitation of Lito Tejada-Flores who told them it would change their lives. They had plans for a quick visit, no more than one day, but after they got there couldn't leave. It was too beautiful. They stayed a week and decided that they wanted their own "piece" of this place. They bought a house in Telluride, with the intent of living there six months of the year and running their Rockcraft courses in the abundantly mountainous surroundings. They took Tamara out of school in winter and enrolled her in school in Telluride.

Like Leysin, Switzerland, Telluride was a scenic and "laid-back" place. But with all its advantages, it was not a suitable place for their type of business. The one small post office was open sometimes and not at other times. After two winters, Liz and Royal decided that it was not going to work. They rented their house in Telluride, using it for summer vacations, and then after ten years sold it.

In 1978, while running the climbing school at Telluride, Royal had a serious attack of psoriatic arthritis. At home in Modesto, he lost much of the use of his right hand. He had to re-learn tennis, using both hands to hold the racket. The arthritis invaded his wrists and ankles and for awhile became so bad that he had trouble walking. He couldn't shake hands and was hardly able to put his hands in his pockets.

He couldn't climb, but the arthritis permitted kayaking. Or as TM Herbert observed, "Royal could keep the pain hidden more easily in kayaking." Rivers had begun to dominate his interests and, fortunately, were an outdoor adventure that he could continue to pursue.

There were parallels to kayaking and climbing. Both required poise, courage, and self-control, plus a strong desire to reach a goal. For one it was the mastery of a stretch of rock, for the other a rapid. The rock was still. Rivers were dynamic and changing. Climbing was methodical and controlled. There was danger, but one could circumvent the danger by actions and thoughts. In kayaking, there rarely were any situations that were black or white. Yet one had to perform correctly--in the middle of power and action.

In the late '70s, Royal almost drowned when the pain of the arthritis was so severe that he was unable to perform an Eskimo roll and tip back up out of the water after capsizing. The arthritis was another huge climb that was going to have to be overcome, somehow, with heart and mind and..., with "faith." Having made so many ideas of climbs turn real, perhaps he could apply his strength and thought to this new summons. Through long-testing of the value of holds, and his own values, and through years where imbalance and stability kept watch on one another, Royal once more had come to an image of the unexpected but the not-altogether insurmountable. As with the upper walls of El Capitan or Half Dome, he would have to throw his hope forward and wait for it to show him the route.

An immense consolation during these years was the excellent, growing relationship Royal had with his father-in-law, Earl Burkner. Royal found in Earl the father he had wanted and referred to him as "Dad." They became as close as any father and son, or any two strong friends, could be. Earl loved Royal's sense of humor. They talked and played games together, everything from cribbage to cork-popping on the dining room table.

196 Earl Burkner with Royal and Liz

XVI

In November, 1979, Liz and Royal's son, Damon, was born.

In 1980, Royal was invited to Chile. His friend, Doug Tompkins, had arranged a river trip down the legendary Bio Bio River for his family and the employees of his firm, Esprit. Doug and Royal would kayak, and the others would descend the cataracts in rafts. A kayak trip to Chile was very questionable, in view of the pain involved for Royal to do an Eskimo roll. As ever, he decided to have faith and go. Perhaps something would happen that was good instead of something bad. If he had the right attitude possibly, if he had faith, things-- perhaps the pain--would change.

To lack faith, from Royal's view, might be visited by other more fearful consequences involving the present and future happiness of the soul. It was written in Emerson's *Self-Reliance* that with the exercise of self-trust new powers appeared. It seemed that Royal was ready again to admit life beyond his power, and knowledge beyond his thoughts, and not blanch or tremble at the risk.

Royal and Doug and a non-kayaking friend, Jim Sims, flew to Chile in six days in Doug's small plane, a Cessna 210. They spent two weeks boating Chilean rivers, making "first descents," one adventure after another. Then they joined their friends and families in Santiago for the journey by auto and train to the Bio Bio.

Liz and eight-year-old Tamara were included in the adventure. This was a class-5 river, and only Royal's respect for the skill of the master boatmen who worked for Sobek River Tours convinced him Tamara would be safe. Damon was left at home in the care of friends. Liz and Royal were enjoying his infancy yet couldn't pass up this trip.

Liz and Tamara rode the river as part of a group in rafts, as Royal and Doug immersed themselves in the huge waves of the river via kayak. The weather was bad, and it was a real test for Tamara. She rose to the occasion and was tough, and cheerful, and spirited throughout the trip. She was destined to become a professional raft-woman herself, taking joy in safely transporting clients through splendid whitewater. There would always remain a spot in her soul marked "Bio Bio." It was her first experience of the majesty of a river. She long would remember the wonderful faces of the people of Chile, including an old man in Santiago who let her sit on his horse (she missed her own). She would remember sitting in the rain, reading a book, the camps along the water, no roads, no bathroom, washing her face in bitingly cold water, cooking breakfast in sunrise, and an episode when the raft Liz was on became stuck in an eddy for a good hour, Tamara watching from the other side of the river and not being able to help....

197 Tamara Robbins at a camp along the Bio Bio, Chile -- photo by Royal Robbins

The trip to Chile was a success, and the change in attitude Royal demanded of himself prior to the trip seemed to initiate a miraculous healing. The arthritis started to leave. It was at this time perhaps that Royal began to believe in miracles, and miracles were happening.

In 1979, Liz started to design clothes. The first of these were the "Billy Goat Shorts," cut for freedom of movement. They became popular and sold well. The business was growing, and it was not long before Royal and Liz would quit the sale of climbing equipment altogether and devote all of their sales to clothing.

The climbing gear brought minor profits compared to the clothes. With climbing gear, they were distributing largely what others had designed and produced. They were thus always in "wars" with other wholesalers who were distributing the same products. With clothing, they had the advantage of Liz's design talents and would sink or swim according to their own creativity. Royal and Liz had suffered a lawsuit when a climber was injured by the failure of a piece of climbing equipment. They won the suit when they were able to establish that the person had misused the gear, but the incident further convinced them of the wisdom of going to clothes solely.

In late summer of '80, Doug Tompkins, Reg Lake, and Royal made the first descent of the San Joaquin River Gorge from Devil's Postpile south of Yosemite to Mammoth Pool Reservoir thirty-two miles to the west and five thousand feet lower. The adventure involved six days of technical paddling through granite-filled terrain of supreme beauty. This traverse marked the introduction into California river-running of a new attitude which Royal called "adventure kayaking." This was a form of descending river canyons more akin to mountaineering than the classic running of rivers. It involved, when necessary, rock climbing and carrying the kayak down terrain too steep to boat. In fact, for its beauty and its feeling of venturing into exciting, new territory, the descent of the San Joaquin River Gorge reminded Royal of the first ascent of the Salathe Wall of El Capitan.

Royal, Doug, and Reg made a good team. Royal had immense respect for both of them. Reg was the most expert kayaker of the group, had a bouyant personality and a warm and witty sense of humor, and also a keen sense of adventure. He was always eager for a challenging river. Royal was the climber of the group and the one who tended to dream up the projects they did together. Doug was the main engine, very aggressive and enterprising. He pushed himself and others to the fine edge more than anyone else Royal had ever seen (and Royal considered this quality to be one of his own). He doubted whether, if Doug hadn't been along, they would have committed themselves to a gorge the passage of which was uncertain and from which retreat would have been exceedingly difficult if not impossible.

In 1981, Liz added shirts to her designs. Whereas Liz had been criticized on occasion for being content to go second on the rope behind the master, she now was visibly in the pilot's role and was, according to Royal, "the leading spirit of the business."

The name of the business was changed from Mountain Paraphernalia to "Royal Robbins." Royal was reluctant to use his name, because "it might lead in the direction of a big head." But his name was well known. By using it, the business would be given "a personality"--particularly in terms of marketing clothing. Royal also realized, with a sense of increased responsibility, that it would show his customers that he stood behind his products. The goal was to measure each design to the specifications of quality, comfort, durability, and a look that had a sense of the earth and a sense of the values of Liz and Royal Robbins.

Summer '81, Doug Tompkins, Reg Lake, and Royal carried their kayaks over snowbound, 13,777-foot Mount Whitney Pass to get to the upper Kern River. Right at the top of the pass, Reg, who was wearing tennis shoes, slipped on the snow and fell seven hundred feet, tumbling over and over with his kayak on his back. Bloody, but not seriously injured, he climbed up again. Royal noted that it was a good thing Reg was dazed from the fall, or he wouldn't have allowed Doug to talk him into climbing back up. They went on to boat fifty-five miles down the Kern Trench, through huge, boulder-strewn rapids. A "first descent," it was an enterprise that captured the awe of the kayaking world.

198 Royal Robbins at 13,777 feet on Whitney Pass enroute to the first descent of the headwaters of the Kern

In 1982, Royal, Doug, and Reg, along with Neusom Holmes, hiked over Bishop Pass and completed their "triple crown" with a first descent of the headwaters of the Middle Fork of the King's River in King's Canyon National Park in the Sierra. This was the largest and steepest river of the three, and the boaters were on "the fine edge" from beginning to end.

199 Neusom Holmes, Doug Tompkins, Reg Lake, Royal Robbins, at a camp on the King's River

In '83, Royal had a close call during a three-week kayak descent of the Tingirirrica River in Chile. The sojourn was another first descent. Approaching a menacing rapid they planned to portage around, Royal waited too long and was swept into the rapid. He was sucked from his boat into a huge "hole," or "keeper," where powerful water recirculated upon itself. He was tossed around, out of control. Each time he struggled toward the surface, he was pulled down. This was bad. This was much worse than it had ever been. A dangerous thought entered his mind, "I'm going to die." He thought this almost calmly, near to complete resignation to a fate of drowning. Then there flashed across his mind a picture of his family: Liz, Tamara, Damon. Something went off inside him. He realized in horror that he was about to surrender, to give up before he was beaten. Instantly, his resolve stiffened. He thought, "No. I haven't drowned yet."

Struggling to the surface, he gulped in air and water, and, choking, was again carried away by the current. He plunged over new drops. Again fighting his way to the surface, he found himself in a small eddy next to a rock wall, exhausted. He tried to swim but was too weak. He was being tugged by the current of the eddy toward the middle of the stream and another wild ride. He reached up and, as the current slowly carried him past the final edge of the rock wall, fitted his fingers onto a small hold on the rock and hung there, careful not to have rushed his grab and missed. He hung there long enough to regain his strength and stumble out of the water.

He had been saved by the thought of his loved ones, when the thought of himself was not strong enough. So in a very real sense, he had been saved by his loved ones--as if they had been there and had pulled him out of the water.

In the same year, 1983, Royal was asked to write an introduction to Layton Kor's autobiography, *Beyond The Vertical*. Commenting on Layton's belief in God, Royal wrote something very beautiful. It had no awkward, philosophical crescendos, and perhaps Royal was expressing something about himself as much as about Layton: "I can imagine that...after he (Layton) had proven himself in so many facets of the climbing world...he looked out and off into the distance, and as far as he could see stretched an endless range of mountains. I can imagine Layton eyeing those peaks receding into infinity and seeing in them insufficient food to satisfy deeper hungers."

In kayaking, as in climbing, fellowship was to Royal an important part of the experience. In this wet sport, he found individuals who, like his climbing friends, were open, large-hearted searchers who burned with passion for their idee fixee. His close friends, Doug Tompkins and Reg Lake were this way, as was Neusom Holmes. They jokingly called their team "the brotherhood" but were aware of the element of truth that lay in that light-hearted phrase. Two of the leading figures of American kayaking, the Californians, Chuck Stanley and Lars Holbek, were similarly filled with this combination of powerful purpose and friendship. Stanley and Holbek vied in a good-natured competition with the "brotherhood" for first descent honors of the dwindling, virgin Sierra Nevada rivers. Occasionally they pooled resources. In 1983, Holbek and Stanley, plus ace boaters John Armstrong and Richard Montgomery, joined Reg and Royal for the first descent of the Tuolumne River from Tuolumne Meadows to Hetch Hetchy Reservoir.

Part of the pleasure of kayaking was, for Royal, to introduce its joys to friends-- Doug Tompkins, Lito Tejadas-Flores, and Yvon Chouinard, for example. Royal taught Lito to ski and also to kayak, and Lito eventually wrote how-to books on both subjects. Lito found Royal to be "...a great mentor, very steady. He has a gift for teaching, patient and logical, qualities which students appreciate in environments that unsettle them." Although bloodied by a nasty swim in the Merced River on one of his early trips, Chouinard bounced right back and soon was looking for first descents himself. He repaid Royal's gift of instruction with a gift of his own, namely the suggestion that they make the first descent of Sespe Creek, a virgin river in southern California.

The Sespe runs through forty miles of wilderness in Los Padres National Forest near Yvon's home in Ventura. Usually only a stream one can walk across, Sespe Creek swells to a mighty torrent following heavy rains. After a big storm in May, 1984, Yvon and Royal, along with Reg Lake, John Wasserman, and Jackson Frishman, boated this river for the first time. They embarked upon this four-day trip with the idea of just getting down somehow and were prepared to carry their boats all the way if necessary. They were delighted to find that they could boat almost the entire distance. The quality of the boating was as good as they had found anywhere, mile after mile of continuous whitewater action, working their way down by darting from the quiet water behind one enormous boulder to the placid water near another.

Royal and Yvon later became involved in efforts to keep this rare wilderness river from being drowned in one more reservoir to slake the Southland's quenchless thirst.

Royal gave the name "flash boating" to this exercise of waiting patiently for the heavens to unleash their bounty and then jumping commando style on the streams while they were high enough to kayak. He used this technique to make the first descents of the Fresno and Chowchilla Rivers and the Middle Fork of the Mokelumne, all Sierra foothills rivers.

In winter of '86, Royal came to Colorado to attend an American Alpine Club meeting in Denver. He valued these occasions of fellowship and gatherings of what he believed were fundamentally decent people. It was good to be with old friends, and he liked to show his support for the good things that the club did for climbing. Despite having in the '60s preferred freedom from any obligations and having suffered in those earlier climbing days from what he called "a retarded development in sociability," he had come to respect the AAC and its people who he found to be energetic and magnanimous. Most of them were, in his view, "...men and women who share a passion for grand vistas and noble actions and are faithful to the ideal that cheap victories are worthless...."

A remarkable number of the greatest individuals in American climbing were at this meeting: Royal, Gill, Kor, Chouinard, Frost, Henry Barber, John Bachar, Fred Beckey, Lynn Hill, Christian Griffith, to name a few, all individuals who had a kindred love of climbing. Layton Kor was the honored guest, and Gill gave a marvelous address. A line stood out from the Gill talk, that he was "never one to be intimidated by the absence of danger."

Several acclaimed traditional climbers were assembled alongside several intense, well-known sport-climbers (who believed in placing bolts by rappel), and the two schools of philosophy engaged in a debate.

Royal commented to me after the debate that John Bachar's traditional approach to climbing, without rappel bolting, was harder. It was "greater." Royal added, "We're going to see new breakthroughs in the traditional approach," and, "It's going to be hard to get looped tonight--these drinks are three dollars a shot."

On Mother's Day, 1987, Royal wrote the following letter:
"Dearest Mother,

The words of any card I could buy could not express the love I have for you. You are simply the greatest mother a son could have. You have made all the difference to me, first because of your faith in me when I was young and troublesome, and later you continue to be a guiding light. Thanks, mom, for being you, for standing by me, for lifting me up, for being an example of the right spirit and of an attitude toward life and toward others that must please God.

I pray that this finds you well, and healthy, and happy. We all look forward to seeing you again soon. Happy Mother's Day.
Your loving son, Royal"

In July of 1988, Royal participated in the first American Bashkaus expedition in Siberia. The U.S.S.R. was one place he had not been, and he and his companions were the first Americans to visit that part of Siberia. The river that they kayaked had been run only by Russians--some of whom had drowned during their attempt.

After not hearing from Royal for many years, Tom Frost received a postcard from Russia with the closing words: "God bless you."

200 American and Russian flags fly together on raft in Siberia

201 Royal resting alongside the river, in Russia

The Vision for Royal and Liz continued to be raising their children, enjoying their children, and operating a successful business. Liz carried on with the designing of clothes, allowing her to achieve beautiful ideas and to enjoy the adventure associated with the development of such insights.

They had bought a cabin in the Sierra an hour and a half east of Modesto, a short distance from Pinecrest Lake, still looking for their ideal home in the mountains away from home. But a smaller cabin in ill-repair in the woods right at the edge of Pinecrest Lake went up for sale. They were attracted to the location next to the lake where they could enjoy both the water and the woods. They mortgaged their house in Modesto to buy it and as soon as possible sold the other cabin and went to work rebuilding the new one. What began as a small remodel became gradually dramatic. Liz did the contracting, chose the wood, thought out every detail of the rooms, and guided the laying of new plumbing and wiring. It became an exquisite place of beauty.

202 Cabin at Pinecrest Lake

Hiking, rock climbing, boating, fishing, biking mountain paths, skiing, cozy nights by the fire, chess, darts, good meals, and time with family typified their visits to the cabin. They spent as many weekends as possible here, often with friends, feeling that this was where their souls were. Tamara joined the ski team at the nearby resort and in her teens quickly became a medalist in ski racing.

The spirit of the cabin was, in a sense, gratitude, its location close to the lake, in the influence of hill, stone, damp scents of a forest floor, the moods of season and time, light trained on its creation, the eternal beauty of the Sierra Nevada. A breeze would spring up and cause huge trunks of pines to sway softly, slowly, outside the windows. It was a place of sanctuary, a place for fostering love, and where they could find quiet--except for the sounds of air high up in the trees, or the laughter of their family, or music from the stereo, or the cracks and pops of wood burning in the fireplace.

203 Liz Robbins and Beulah Chandler at Pinecrest

It was their hope to try to translate these aspects of life into the feel of their clothing products. They wanted what they sold to reflect how they lived, clothes connected somehow to the fabric of the inner spirit. Shirts had to have the colors of the mountains and rivers. Their goal was to imitate the integrity of nature's forms.

A September '88 *America West Airlines Magazine* reported, in a story about Royal, that his commercial undertaking of clothing was grossing $10 million a year. Yet Royal was not turning into a supercilious entrepreneur. He seemed to be growing more human, more compassionate and understanding, and was having simpler, perhaps more human, experiences--such as working with kids as a member of the Modesto Soccer Association or having Boy Scouts visit the cabin and taking them climbing. Royal felt that he owed a life-long debt to the Boy Scouts. They had first gotten him into the out-of-doors and opened his awareness to the beauty of nature and the thrill of outdoor action.

The person characterized in the '60s by Tom Patey as having a "Sphinx-like inscrutability" was more than ever truly a human being, in contrast to his "superhuman" life. His view of the world was born out of the vast matrix of experience that had made him, yet his knowledge and growth and reflection had culminated in an astute, current appreciation.

In a newspaper article in the Modesto paper, Royal rather glibly stated that he never did perfect climbing or get anywhere near as good at climbing as he felt he wanted to be. In an interview in *Summit Magazine*, in winter 1988, he reflected about climbing. It had given him something on which to focus, he said. "When you have something to focus on, then you're more alive and you're doing what we're here to do, what we're meant for."

The same words were appropriate also, perhaps, for kayaking. By now Royal had made the first descents of the headwaters of a number of rivers in the Sierra and more than a dozen first descents in Chile. In 1989, he wrote a warm, unaffected story, with no strained diction, in the book *First Descents--In Search Of Wild Rivers*, edited by Cameron O'Connor and John Lazenby. The fresh quality of the writing strangely reminded a reader of the spirit of the early days of climbing in Yosemite. There existed the same fear, the same joy of adventure, the friendship, the waterfalls, views of sunlit, white, Sierra granite, and, as Royal wrote, "the same awestruck wonder at the glory of the handiwork of God."

The riches of kayaking included the beauty of river canyons, the changing light, the rocks, getting lost from his friends, and spending the night alongside roads in South America. It included wonderful food and riverside camps, or famous post-trip meals prepared by Liz. Kayaking was sipping vodka with Russians and going to the Russian circus. It was watching for an eddy line that marked opposing currents. Kayaking was the steely concentration evoked by a rapid, and looking into the beyond when sucked into one. The boundless beauty of a sun casting its final light across South American mountains at the end of a day became combined with the terror of an oncoming hydraulic.

204 Kayaking through rapids

Royal learned the same respect for rapids as he had for rock climbs and demonstrated the same mastery of peer pressure. He was not too proud to portage around a rapid that a friend would run. In a way, kayaking required more courage for Royal than climbing. The commitment to a rapid involved fewer choices, and no feeling of being able to turn back. Occasionally the rugged terrain of a river involved climbing, roping their boats up and down granite walls. Through the eyes of business-tycoon and "environmental philanthropist" Doug Tompkins: "Royal was not a world-class kayaker. He would be more accurately described as a very good adventure boater. He's not a great athlete. But he applied his skills in climbing to kayaking. He took the big-wall mentality to rivers. He studied the problem and extended the vision of what could be done, going high into the Sierras, climbing up with the boat on his shoulders, and kayaking where white-water champion boaters thought you couldn't get along. Royal was always thinking."

Royal recognized kayaking as a frontier nearly equal to the unclimbed Yosemite walls of the '50s. As in climbing, he found himself a bit obsessed: studying maps, determining with a calculator the vertical drop per mile of a river, and planning helicopter approaches to difficult put-ins. Adventure was, and had been for a long time, his way of life.

205 Damon Robbins, with paddle -- photo by Royal Robbins

254

206 Royal Robbins -- photo by Will Mosgrove

Queried as to whether adventure kayaking meant as much to him as climbing, Royal replied, "No. I love it very much, and it is very rewarding, but I am first, last, and always a climber. I will climb until I drop, and it would be the last thing I would give up."

In May of '90, while in Italy for the Trento Film Festival, Royal did a little climbing on a limestone cliff. He found that he was not very strong and not too effective on rock. He was not in great climbing shape, but--compared to when he had arthritis--to be able to climb at all was important. Time seemed to be undoing a few of the ravages of age.

XVII

"Where the spirit does not work with the hand, there is no art."-- Leonardo Da Vinci.

Throughout the '80s, there was a crusade in the climbing world toward "sport-climbing"--an attempt to expand the possibilities for first ascents, a new, more overtly competitive--but in many ways less valiant--mentality where the drilling of bolts was considered welcome rather than to be avoided. Climbers were increasing in number rapidly, and talented individuals wanted to assert their individuality.

Indoor, artificial climbing walls sprang up everywhere, and climbing competitions on these walls were occurring with surprising popularity. These artificial walls were the more intelligent side of sport-climbing, providing an arena for training or competition and offering a fun, social occasion for an evening--such as in England where visits to the climbing wall began to replace visits to the pub. Artificial walls provided needed relief for the natural rock formations but also encouraged the onslaught of the general populace in climbing. Rock gyms replaced fitness centers, and Wall Street executives could climb cliffs without leaving the comfort of their clubs. Safety harnesses, air conditioning, neon tights.... Climbing was, in essence, made "safe" and "popularized" for mass consumption, carrying with it all of the markings of fashion.

An aberration of sport-climbing, or perhaps its wicked soul, was "rappel bolting"--a process in opposition to the "canon," as it were, of climbing where routes were done from the ground up. Individuals started doing new routes from the top down. This involved rappelling a short, unclimbed wall and drilling a line of bolts that the imagined route would follow. It involved previewing the handholds and practicing individual moves of the proposed climb while hanging on the rope. It involved hanging on each bolt to rest or to work out an individual move (called "hangdogging"). For a few people, it consisted of carving, chipping, drilling, or gluing holds if there were not already enough God-given holds in existence on that specific surface of rock.

Beautifully-sculpted rock was sacrificed to power-drills, and there became less and less of the underlying "reverence" climbers such as Royal felt was owed to the mountains and to nature.

Climbing magazines began to hype the most talented of these athletes who were establishing routes by bolting on rappel. Always answering to the persuasions of the media, the herds took up the cause. New lines were bolted sometimes as near as two to three feet from other routes that could be protected easily with nuts. Bolts were placed on rappel by unknowing climbers down routes that had previously been climbed from the ground up without bolts! Routes were created that had been left undone for years by traditional climbers whose sensibilities dictated that too many bolts would be required for those routes.

Whereas bolts once had been placed while standing in balance, sometimes while only on tiny footholds, and tapping with a hammer for half an hour on a small, hand-held drill, there were suddenly power drills that made bolting virtually effortless. When bolts had been difficult to place, a climber was less inclined to put them in too often or where they were not absolutely necessary. If the climbing was too tenuous to let go to place a bolt, the route was overcome with courage or was left undone. Leaving specific climbs "undone" was an art. It was necessary. Such self-imposed limits, and unknowns, gave to climbing a sense of fairness. These were limits designed to preserve a spirit of integrity in climbing.

But now every remaining pristine surface of unclimbed rock was going to be forced, since it could be conveniently pre-protected by rappel and since the new world order was hungry to enlarge its domain. There would be no shortage of climbing, but also less adventure. Climbers needed only to purchase a power drill and stake their claim. Power drills were not restricted to experts. Relative beginners and mediocre climbers also started to come armed with power devices in the hope of following in the example of their heroes, those rap-bolters glorified by the climbing magazines.

In the spirit of this mania, climbers started getting more and more casual as to where they thought bolts should go. In Tuolumne, climbers added bolts to more than one section of rock that Royal had led the first ascent of without a bolt. On one such route--a long, scary runout--a bolt was added by climbers simply to eliminate the factor of fear. In turn, that bolt was chopped by John Bachar who during the '80s was perhaps the best of the new athletes in rock climbing and who defended the traditional, "ground up" style of doing first ascents. He detested the adding of bolts to existing routes.

Bachar and I one day did that Tuolumne climb of Royal's, called "Gray Ghost," and Bachar expressed his feelings on the subject: "Robbins is a master climber, and then they go up and try to destroy something that he did that was great...." Bachar was a leader among the new generation's super-climbers and believed in the legacy of the revered spirits who were his predecessors.

207 John Bachar in Tuolumne -- photo by Pat Ament

From Royal's point of view, Bachar climbed "in the tradition of the outstanding visionaries before him, such as Henry Barber." Barber, according to Royal, "had a high sense of style--a style in keeping with the principle that getting to the top is nothing and how you do it is everything."

208 Hot Henry Barber -- photo by Pat Ament

Barber's record-time solo of the Salathe-Steck route on Sentinel (in less than three hours) was an illustration of his "active vision." Bachar carried such vision even further, with extreme free-solo ascents. In Royal's words, "You have to admire the great art that Bachar has displayed in his soloing."

The majority of the oblivious masses had no express malice toward traditional climbers, but there were other fervent despoilers with the direct intent of dismantling the traditions Royal had helped to establish. When John Bachar and other traditionalists throughout the country began, in protest, to "chop" (remove) rappel-placed bolts, the war was on.

Many climbers turned and became outspoken apostates of their own earlier traditional approaches, describing the rappel-bolting they were now doing as valid and revolutionary. This was at times a spirit suffused with a rage. Bolters were inflamed that anything should get between the rock and their drilling as they pleased. This wrath now and then found its expression in violence, such as tire-slashings and actual physical attacks on climbers suspected of being covert bolt-choppers. John Bachar was engaging in a somewhat caustic discussion in Yosemite with two rap-bolters when one, without warning, physically assaulted him.

Royal viewed this as a type of terrorism by the new against the old. Once a relatively homogeneous and companionable group, climbers had become violently disparate. Besides the contrasting philosophies of climbers, powerful business interests and money were now involved. Catering to the mob, climbing-equipment companies were happy to see trends that reduced climbing to a common denominator whereby every person with any money could be a paying customer of climbing.

It was ironic that the "old guard," those with anti-bolt values, who once were viewed as a peculiar people outside the mainstream of society, were now thought of as freaks outside of climbing.

Finally, in an article, Royal condemned the new practices as they applied in Yosemite and other strongholds of traditional American rock climbing. He called rap-bolters "vandals in the temple." *Climbing Magazine* refused to publish the article, because it was "too controversial," but it was published reluctantly by *Rock N' Ice Magazine*.

At first, Royal suggested stopping the use of bolts altogether but then revised his message to say that he had no beef with rap-bolting in areas suited to it, particularly areas not otherwise developable, such as crackless cliffs or cliffs of poor rock. But he was against adding bolts to climbs to make them easier or safer and was against rap-bolting in areas where their existed a non-rap-bolting tradition, such as in Yosemite and Tuolumne.

His interest was not in repressing the creativity of a new generation, or doubting their physical abilities, but rather in being a conduit for a continuing definition of true creativity in rock climbing. He felt that these "anguish-free" approaches destroyed what would be test pieces for tomorrow's climbers. Rap-bolting "stole routes from the future." It seemed to Royal supremely arrogant to think that we could dream of the limits of the master climbers of the future. And it seemed selfish to be so covetous of route-bagging that rappel-bolting should be so very necessary.

Rap-bolting did make for hundreds of excellent new routes, transforming blank rock into small wonders of free-climbing workability, yet imposing upon the outdoors an artificiality that was more appropriate to the gyms. People could create athletic feats--but at the expense of the exploratory aspects of an adventure ethic, that engagement with the unknown, with uncertainty, according to Royal.

As removed from the mainstream of climbing as Royal was, he found himself suddenly in another controversy--with bolts at its center. In the Rock N' Ice article, he said that unlimited bolting was going to be a kind of "end of the world" for rock climbing.

Great people are disturbers. They shake you and threaten you with small, eternal truths. Yet many of the newer climbers had not even heard of Royal's name or were vaguely aware of the magnitude of his accomplishments. Many of the developing generation had no interest in history and were, almost by the dictates of an increasingly competitive and self-focused culture, ambivalent to heritage. To be told suddenly that where they were going might be a step backwards, was hard on the new, young, trail blazers.

Flashy youngsters wished that this specter from the past would mind his business. His themes distracted them from The World Cup. Royal did not need to be condemned for staying true to his centers and to his earliest feelings. What might he have done had he rap-bolted or had he tried routes a hundred times, or had he...? I'd seen 5.12 climbers of the modern era struggle at their limits--with the protection of a bolt at eye level--to lead Royal's 1964, chalkless, boltless, runout, no-sticky-shoe-rubber, 5.11 lead "on sight" of the first pitch of Athlete's Feat in Boulder Canyon. In 1985, Patrick Edlinger--one of Europe's top climbers--took three tries to do a section of rock that Robbins did in one try in 1964.

A few of those climbers who were the most anarchic or who were unwilling to anastomose with the past, who refused to have passed onto them the values of a previous generation, came forward with surprising hatred of Royal. They expressed their desire, in fact, to preside over the destruction of the previous "ethic." They were not ignorant of the past but were willfully throwing it away. With sport-climbers now the largest body of the readership of the larger climbing magazines, and with sport-climbing receiving the most frequent sponsorship from businesses, it was necessary for editors to give equal (actually more) time to the rap-bolting side of the argument. Several pages of an issue of Rock N' Ice were given to one climber who wrote a vindictive treatise on Royal, painting him as a has-been and an old, spiritual philosopher of climbing. The commentary was entitled *Robbins--No Longer Royal.*

It seemed accurate to observe that the most vehement detractors of Royal had not as yet themselves made any sort of contribution in climbing that was likely to be remembered. Nor had the majority of the rap-bolting contingent. But Royal would be remembered. Their intimacy with rock, their devotion to the art of climbing, was, with everything said and done, minor compared to his. He simply had more to tell than anyone else about rock climbing--however "out of touch with the times" many sport-climbers insisted he was.

It was Royal's feeling that a few of these rap-bolters were in fact cowards at the core, unable to approach the level of achievement of the modern traditionalists who were continuing to be the keepers of the flame--Henry Barber and David Breashears in the '70s and then John Bachar, Peter Croft, and Derek Hersey, to name a few spirits of the 1980's and early '90s whose achievements, Royal felt, were leaving his and everyone's in the dust.

210 Peter Croft and Royal Robbins -- photo by Pat Ament

Realizing the ultimate futility of his written remarks and the defiance of rap-bolters (most were unmovable in the opinion that their approach was superior), Royal decided to stop arguing and rather turn his energies toward celebrating those expressions of adventure that were in keeping with what he saw as timeless values of courage, vision, craft, self-discipline, and love of the sport.

As a small irony of the time, Warren Harding was on a climbing slide-show tour and invariably included in his talks a great deal of praise for Royal. He had almost always kept his resentment disguised and, in the face of Royal's criticisms, had in the past the good grace to characterize himself as "the devil." At one of these lectures, in Boulder, Colorado, I listened to Harding say, "I might have had a basis to argue some of Royal's philosophies, but for the fact that he was such a dang much better climber than I."

211 "the Devil" (Warren Harding) and "God" (Royal Robbins),
at Reno trade show, 1991

In spring 1991, Royal was honored as guest speaker for the National
British Mountaineering Conference in Buxton, England. "I went over to help Ken
Wilson defend traditional climbing," he said to me with a smile. By the approval
of the large audience, Royal and Ken won the debate hands down. Their sport-
climbing counterparts had not thought through their arguments.

While in England, Royal soloed a few moderate English rock climbs with Ken. At one point, too high above the ground to hazard a fall, Royal's hand strength almost gave out. From a stance above, Ken reached down and extended a hand that might be grabbed in the event Royal should fall. At the last second, Royal was able to get a hold and move back down without using the hand.

Ken Wilson offers a few memories of Royal's visit to England:

"In the Buxton debate, the gulf between Royal and me and Jerry Moffat and Chris Gore was enormous. It wasn't so much that they thought bolting was OK and we didn't, but it was more the total lack of theology in their argument and approach. It was summed up for me by Moffat's comment that if a route had six bolts and one nut placement he would be quite happy to replace that nut with a bolt to make a nice, good, fun, no-complication route. The argument should be that they would defend that nut placement to the death and seek to remove another bolt in favor of a nut. Moffat and Gore came along blissfully unprepared, because they didn't care. They want climbing to be a free-for-all, ethics don't matter anymore. Sure we won the debate (battle), but the war is already lost. Royal and I were like zealous legionnaires trying to defend an outpost of the Roman empire when the whole core of the empire had gone soft. It was notable in that Catherine Destivelle had the character to stand up and be counted, to complain about the rapacious bolting around Chamonix--often on rock with plenty of nuttable cracks. Catherine has within her some strain of romance, the same thing that moved Royal in his formative days, as if she is searching for some great test, some destiny within the mountains. While climbing at the Roaches, Royal displayed tremendous steadiness and competence. He was unfit for climbing, with weak fingers, etc., so we rapidly lapsed into easy soloing of which there is quite a lot (with excellent quality), some of it with spectacular, life-threatening positions. All the conference luminaries had gone there, and we were soloing among them--a business not usually to Royal's taste (he likes to be discreet). Thus I had to be careful with Royal's image. It wouldn't have done to have been seen being incompetent on anything too hard. So we soloed routes I knew well but he (weak and cautious) did not. He was, I eventually realized, finding it quite taxing. But throughout, he conducted himself with that steady precision, never a rushed move, never a wobble or a tremor, always dignity and serenity. I'd had a similar day a few years earlier with Cassin and observed the same steadiness and precision. Later in the day, Royal and I roped up and did a famous climb--Valkyrie (5.7)--with a friend who was awestruck to be within twenty feet of the charismatic and not unattractive Catherine Destivelle. So when he found himself roped up to an all-time God like RR, it was something of a shock. The other day, this friend applied for membership in the Alpine Club. I noted his pride in entering on his very modest list of climbs the fact that he had done Valkyrie with RR (and, incidentally, a very good time we had too)."

XVIII

Tim Shultz, Steve Brawley, and I spent a week in Yosemite in late June of '91 and then were invited to Royal's home in Modesto, California. Royal suggested that we could climb on a rock formation he recently discovered not far from his cabin on Pinecrest Lake.

In Modesto, we entered a different, larger house than I had visited before. It had been the home of Liz's parents and was purchased by Royal and Liz, a house of Spanish, Mediterranean style.

Liz prepared dinner with her usual skill. I chopped red onions and parsley for her to mix with steamed potatoes. She softened some bok choy in a wok. The bok choy was then combined with lightly cooked spinach. A salad made of growings from the backyard garden and newly picked California plums were additional courses. Liz spoke lovingly to one of their parakeets. It gave her a tiny peck-kiss. Liz was worried that their cat, Cricket, hadn't come home last night. Damon, now eleven years old, chased another cat, Tux, from a distance with a remote control car. Tamara was away--guiding raft trips down the American River near Placerville, California. Liz let me stroke one of two small, pet snakes which she lifted gently out of a sand aquarium. The latest addition to the house, a puppy by the name of Betty, seemed happy but slightly lost amid these festivities.

At the start of the meal, Royal offered a short blessing of thanks. This was provocative and surprised me. I hadn't seen him do that before. We enjoyed the meal and discussed climbing, where it had evolved, how climbing was a means by which people learn and grow throughout their lives. Royal reflected that human progression was the real theme of climbing. "You start over here in the mud, and then you go somewhere, you have something--a little order or structure, and wisdom. You have friends, an identity, and experience."

We sat at a long, wooden table. The room was oblong and spacious, with white, textured walls. The floors were wood, and there were almost wall-high windows that let in bright, friendly light. Royal sipped wine and thought stoically.

In the morning, as Royal, Tim, Steve, and I prepared to depart for the mountains, Liz requested that I not push Royal on the rock too hard. Liz and I hugged, and I snapped a photo of her, Royal, and Damon.

212 Liz, Royal, Damon, and Betty -- photo by Pat Ament

Tim and Steve drove my car, and I rode with Royal. We stopped at a market where Royal picked up more plums. He brought his own mesh bag into the store. He hadn't used a paper or plastic bag in a year, one small demonstration of his commitment to the environment.

During the couple of hours it took to drive to Sonora, Royal and I spoke on many topics. I was surprised by things he said that I was already feeling privately in my own inner theater. He told me about the crag we were headed for near Sonora, the location of which he was guarding, and the new routes he judged might exist on it. He described a dream he had years ago in which he happened upon the consummate crag, a Shangri-la of unclimbed rock with a road weaving along the rock's base. "I guess I've been on a kind of hunt for the perfect crag for years," he mused. It was clear that he was delighted now to be on the way to climb, although he delivered a warning similar to the one Liz gave. "I would guess that my climbing level now is about 5.8." Aware of the experience and technique that he had, I did not believe this assessment to be true.

As we drove, Royal pointed to an old horse that stood rigidly on a hill. Its head was drooped down almost to the ground. The horse had stood in that favorite place for years, overlooking the road. "A newspaper did an article on him," Royal said. "His name is Cricket."

Along the drive, Royal told a story about Tom Frost. Near the top of the first ascent of the North America Wall of El Capitan, in 1964, it was Tom's turn to lead. But Tom stated that he didn't feel well. He gave the lead to Royal. Much later, it occurred to Royal that Tom felt fine that day but had decided that the climb was Royal's idea and that Royal should make it to the top first. Royal offered this evidence to me of the kind of person Frost was. Frost later said that Royal was wrong in this. Tom confessed that he had finally reached the point of being overcome mentally by the strain of that huge climb, but that it was the variety of integrity Robbins possessed to give a friend the benefit of the doubt.

Royal slowed the car as we approached a bridge. He gazed below at a river and noted that the water was too low now probably to kayak. He told of an occasion when he was kayaking that river and hit a rock. "I broke five ribs."

We pulled off onto and followed an old, narrow, abandoned dirt road. Royal stopped at a break in the trees and pointed to a very weird edifice of gray-red-green-white-and-black, volcanic rock. Tim, Steve, and I had a few doubts that Royal was going to here find something in the way of a total crag. At a wide place in the road, we parked, clipped a few carabiners and nuts together, shouldered three ropes, and started upward through forest. Above the trees, slopes of rock were overgrown with flowers from late spring rain. We pushed our way up through stiff, crackly, oak bushes, at the mercy of Royal's caprice. Yet the day--full of sun and clear blue sky, a soft, cool wind, the quiet, and views of endless Sierra--made me think of Joseph Conrad's remark, "Woe to the man whose heart has not learned while young to hope, to live, to love--and to put its trust in life."

Royal gave me the first lead. Moss grew over some of the initial rock and peeled off in hand and underfoot. It required care to prevent your peeling away with it into space.

At first the rock was shattered, holds balanced in wobbly stacks like bricks. If you weren't sure of a hold, you threw it off and found one that was better underneath. The quiet of the area was occasionally interrupted by the clack of a bricklike hold thrown down. The goal was to establish a general line through these loose poetries toward what appeared to be more solid stuff above. I examined and re-examined holds and interpreted their and my needs. I placed protection frequently.

Things would upon occasion become very silent, as if we were projecting our thoughts above. Several blackbirds and a hawk circled above the forest in the distance. We were happy, fixed with an idea, the first involvement with a crag that had not been climbed. If the rock happened to be loose to this point, who cared? It was climbing. It was a resplendent day. And no one wanted to ruin Royal's hopes about Shangri-la.

He chuckled at himself, at his trying to make the grotesque conform to his fantasies. In a way, this was something he had attempted to do all his career as a climber: to bring a strength to the focus of people around him and a credit to his and their reality. His was a quality of leadership that still was inspiring. As always, we, his friends, struggled against it, or else we followed.

Royal led up the second rope length. As much as hands on holds, the wrestle was--for Royal and me--that of age. I, for one, felt as rigid as that horse on the hill. Royal spoke about how it hurt a little to sit on the belay ledge, how he had to shift his position. We chatted about the uncertainty, the apprehension, the pleasure, of going up on steep, unfamiliar rock. Youthful invincibility, with enough years, was replaced by reflection. Royal had something that was superior to physical brawn: a passing through him of years of climbing and what those years were explaining to him now of his world and his life.

Tim and Steve were content to allow us to reclaim the savor of a bygone era, however worthy or unworthy our glory was at this point in time. The three allowed me the next lead. I left them on a meager ledge where they participated in a talkfest. I moved cautiously, with no particular urgency. The rock was more and more defined, our deliverance visible now by way of a fifty-foot, vertical-- maybe slightly overhanging--dihedral. I began up it without thinking and met with climbing more severe than anticipated. I deliberated out loud. "I'm going to move back down a bit and think about this." Royal replied, "Yeah, Pat, why don't you move back down a bit and think about it." I heard the laughter of three, fifty feet below.

He was by turns serious, ribald, reflective, or silly. I visualized the moves of the dihedral and then climbed it: a few awkward stems (one behind the back), a saving, hidden, three-finger hole, and lichen in my eyes. I could hear Royal huff, as I belayed him up. "That's about my limit," he said. His "limit" was higher now than he had said.

Along the top, we found a way through more oak bushes, past a massive juniper, to where the crag was shorter and it was possible to rappel to the scree and oak below. Royal rappelled first. By the time Tim, Steve, and I finished the rappel, Royal had soloed a forty-foot chimney and was downclimbing broken rock to its right. Royal had joked that he wanted to mark the crag as his own by doing a few new routes, "...the way a dog wets on a fire hydrant." The remainder of the hike down was spent thinking of names for our climb... "The Lifted Leg," "I've Fallen, And I Can't Get Up...." We laughed at just about anything. Driving toward Royal's cabin, he suggested we have dinner across the lake at a restaurant called "the Steam Donkey." I misheard and restated it as "the Steamed Donkey." Royal guffawed and admonished me that, "...people take their donkeys seriously out here." The name of our climb would become "the Esteemed Donkey."

From the cabin, Royal boated us across Pinecrest Lake. He took a long, circular way around so that we could enjoy the lake and see the shoreline houses. The sun was setting. Fish mouths made hundreds of small ripple-circles on the surface of the water. The boat was small. As Royal stood up in it to get better views, the sides tipped within inches of the water. On a nearby shore were several granite boulders where Royal occasionally climbed or had taught climbing.

We arrived at a small marina and left the boat, a short walk to the Steam Donkey. When a waitress set a large, round, hot loaf of bread on our table, Royal said, "Let's break bread together. That's what friends should do." It was in part our light mood that motivated the comment, but the words also elicited a deeper relevance.

When we returned to the marina, the boat was gone. Steve had forgotten to tie it. We looked for it in the dark. The boat had, by luck, parked itself a short distance away, against the dock. Royal announced that Steve had forfeited his ride in the boat and would now have to swim.

In the darkness, staring at the full firmament, as we boated back across the lake, I felt Royal's presence, a man who was playful and who was serious-- reflection was not inconsistent with high spirits. Staring into the infinitude of sky, I felt that this trip across the lake refined for me the best that Royal and I had accumulated in the way of friendship through the years.

As we approached the shore, he stood up again in the boat and tipped it from side to side--the rest of us clutching the gunwales. Outside the cabin in darkness, we had to watch for shoe-size holes in the ground that Damon had dug as "traps for people." With a fire blazing in the fireplace, we played darts and chess. Royal was proud of his dart proficiency and made sport of the rest of us.

He had followed my chess activities and wanted to play me. We lost ourselves in a game. A compact disc recording of *The Greatest Hits of Bob Dylan* added to this quiet, good time. "Let's face it," Royal said at one point, "Dylan is the best. You said that a long time ago, Pat, and you were right." I remembered that Royal had in 1964 introduced me to the music of Dylan.

213 Royal analyzes the situation, at Pinecrest, Summer 1991
-- photo by Pat Ament

At about one-thirty in the morning, we all turned in from fatigue. The sun came up, and we were awakened by a phone call from Liz. Royal and Liz were trying to arrange a location near Pinecrest Lake for an upcoming sales representatives meeting. Royal was amused as he told me that the theme of the meeting this year was going to be "Heroes." His clothing business had the slogan, "style with mountaineering heritage."

It was difficult for me to gauge the business part of Royal. I had only outside indications with which to imagine: the phone in his car, the exquisite livability and size of both his house and cabin, the rare paintings on walls, and on shelves artifacts that he and Liz had collected from around the world. As with anything that he pursued, his business functioned--I imagined--on a higher order of integrity than the norm.

Before leaving to climb again, Royal asked for another game of chess. "I never let anyone beat me twice," he vowed, coming on as though serious. Tim and Steve worked at their darts.

A short drive took us to several large, vibrant granite boulders that offered a number of top-rope ascents. Royal ran impishly all over the rock, up, down, across.

He had no hesitation on a slippery, 5.10 hand crack--his "limit" was continuing to rise. I took a photo of him being a ham on one of the summits. He pointed out a shallow, deceptively moderate-looking crack he hadn't felt the confidence yet to attempt. I managed the crack my first try and felt that it was 5.11a. My forearm tightened at one move and quivered. Royal watched as Tim and Steve wrestled with the crack. When they both at last drew from themselves a sequence, Royal decided he could not be left out. He turned to me and said, "I guess I'm just going to have to climb this."

Remembering the tricks Royal had, in the way of technique, was like a classifying of the intelligences. A thumb contorted in opposition to a finger. His left foot pressed behind him, with heel up in the air, on an elusive, upside-down-slanting hold. His placing of the edges of his shoes was intimation of years of test piece ascents. His limit now, at age fifty-six, was 5.11a.

214 Royal on 5.11a crack near Pinecrest
-- photo by Pat Ament

As though to make conversation, I analyzed how the crack had looked easy from a distance and that I'd expected to have no trouble. The difficulty had taken me by surprise. My body had not been fed the kind of information to help it realize that it was going to have to perform a feat. As a result, the climb turned out to be more than it should have. "What you mean to say is that you were not mentally prepared," was Royal's rejoinder. He waited patiently, alertly, for his opportunities. In general he was ready to call you to accountability for anything you said, but the spirit emanating from him now was more genial, more caring, than in former years. He and Liz had traveled in human distance, since the '60s.

I mockingly took on the visage of interviewer. "Tell us, Mr. Robbins, why you have decided to get back into climbing with such a vengeance."

"I hate youth!"

With my hands on the first holds of a round, vertical, imposing corner of granite, I no longer felt motivated and uttered a few usually dependable apologies. "I feel very lazy and weak all of a sudden. This route is probably too hard for the shape I'm in. I don't think my aging bones should be expected to go through these kinds of struggles anymore."

Royal replied: "So if I've got it right, if you fail it will be because of weakness due to lassitude, it will be because the route is too hard, because you're out of shape, and you're too old, but it won't be because of you." Direct, smart aleck, he knew how to alight upon the nerve that was exposed or the funny bone. We laughed together, and I went up the holdless obelisk somehow. As I stepped into the decisive move, Royal said, "That's a great piece of climbing." Never in my memory had Royal withheld praise, while at the same time he was instant at intruding into your transparencies.

It was the hour for Tim, Steve, and me to return to Colorado, time for Royal to go his way. He acknowledged Tim and Steve for their attitudes, their cheerful, level outlook on life. Royal then stared into my spirit as though he had become conscious of me in the way that I wished to be known. In that glance and in the statement "We'll be in touch," he instilled in me a part of what I lacked: an assurance, and personal esteem. Tim took a photo of Royal and me. Royal slung an arm around my shoulder. "Comrade style," he said. Only an artist of these surroundings could speak with that much light.

XIX

In October of '91, Royal invited me to come to Modesto and attend, as his guest, a seminar that he was helping to facilitate. He and Liz had attended the Pacific Institute seminar in Seattle and felt that they were given a refreshing, energizing education. Royal described it as "strong, powerful material based on state-of-the-art psychology." The aim of the instruction, by Pacific Institute founder Lou Tice, was a modest one: self-growth and increased personal effectiveness through an improved understanding of the processes of thought and by learning how to remove subconscious impediments. Just as Royal had recognized the genius of TM Herbert or John Gill, so did he see Lou Tice as an important minister to the mental well-being of the world.

Royal also included with the invitation to the seminar the possibility that I write his biography, a secret hope of mine for years. As though he knew my spirit, he gave to me--by this bombshell--the life-affirming jolt of my dreams.

Royal, Liz, Damon, I, and Monique--a young, classical voice student from Switzerland who was staying with them--enjoyed a warm, friendly week together in Modesto. We listened to the soothing, mysterious music of Enya. Tamara was in Greece, in her first year of university study which included a course in the anthropology of religion. She had placed herself away from the comfort and modern conveniences of home. Despite such things as no water for taking showers and a diet to which she was having difficulty adjusting, she was determined to finish the course. I sensed that Tamara had all of Royal's drive and intensity and also the same toughness sometimes in dealing with people. Royal told me that she had a dislike of superficial conversation, materialism, hypocrisy, and anything that she detected was phony.

For three days, we let Lou Tice plant in us the seeds of explosive, personal growth. Liz and Royal approached the Pacific Institute information almost as a religion, finding hope in it for their own progression and also for the improvement of attitudes in their business.

Other nights, Royal and I had lengthy, inspired talks about life. He had no more arthritis now, except in one finger, and was counting himself very blessed. "I feel that I have a whole new set of years now to live and enjoy," he said. He still held his tennis racket, however, with two hands.

I slept in Tamara's room. Hanging on a mirror were a number of medals she had won ski racing. There were photos on the wall of her jumping horses. She was formally attired in the photos, a somewhat skilled equestrian. A story by TM Herbert had circulated in the climbing community of Royal's newfound, Christian "authoritarianism," how Royal had not wanted Tamara to ride her horse on Sundays. Neither Royal nor Tamara could remember this ever being the case, however. When I asked Royal about the story, he chuckled and imagined how TM would be able to take a rumor such as that and turn it into something hilarious.

Royal spoke to me of how much he and Liz loved Tamara and Damon. They planned to spend the upcoming Christmas together in Italy.

Halloween night, Royal and Liz were going to a party as the cowardly lion and Dorothy (from the Wizard Of Oz). It was wonderful to see Royal in that costume, with big, furry feet. This was something Royal might not have done in earlier years. But now he enjoyed pushing his "comfort zones" in many directions. Damon's idea of halloween was to dress in a black Ninja suit, climb and hide behind trees, jump out at me, yell, and attempt to kick me.

Royal and Liz had always been creatively happy in their shared life, but their out-reaching interest in human happiness and the radiance of their energy were never more in contagious evidence. It was hard to keep up with them.

Royal employed some of his energy on what he called "the Yosemite course." Certain days, he would leave Modesto at nine a.m., drive at the speed limit to Yosemite, solo a moderate climb up and down, drop his kayak at El Portal along the Merced River, drive twelve miles down the road along the river to a point of take-out, park his car, hitchhike back to his kayak, run the twelve miles of river, and then drive at the speed limit back to Modesto in time for a tennis foursome at five-thirty p.m.

Given a choice, of course, he preferred to be on the weaker team in tennis, since a positive outcome was less certain but more rewarding. In his fifties, Royal was still a mad rebel. He would later write and tell me how, on an impulse, he tromped cross-country to his cabin from the ski area, a struggle of nine continuous hours through forest and deep snow.

Another night, Royal and Liz seemed exhausted from a day of business meetings. Fully clothed and meditative, they collapsed side by side on their bed and discussed which of them would go to an upcoming meeting in Hong Kong. It had been a busy month that included a climbing rescue near Pinecrest, where a young climber had broken a lot of bones in a nasty fall down a cliff. Fortunately for the climber, Royal was nearby--at the granite boulders--and supervised a complicated rescue. Royal's picture was published in the Modesto paper. He was a hero once more.

They also honored him at the Modesto Rotary Club. A member of the club, he told me something of what it meant to be a Rotarian. It was the largest service-oriented organization of its kind in the world, with a million and a quarter members, an association of community leaders and individuals who were leaders in their own professions. There were two purposes of the organization: fellowship and good works in the community or the world at large. For him there were additional purposes: to do something different and to challenge his comfort zones. Liz's father, Earl, had been a member of the Modesto club, and Royal was in part inspired to become a member by his respect for Earl.

215 Royal speaks at the Rotary Club, in Modesto

While Royal and Liz were at work during the day, I friendshipped the cats and walked the puppy, Betty. I visited the Royal Robbins store. He and Liz had structured the entire business around environmental concerns and gave ten percent of their proceeds to environmental projects. Employees were paid extra for days they rode their bikes to work. Clothes were made with only natural fibers, and plastic buttons were not used. Shirts instead had Tagua buttons, made from a nut that grows on trees in Ecuador. In a small way, these buttons contributed to the livelihood of the natives but also to the preservation of the rain forests. Labels on Robbins garments had various environmental messages, such as: "The fight to save the Earth is everyone's concern...." I was told by an employee that the business recycled everything possible and that they were working to get other businesses to do the same.

To share with me a little of the philosophy of the company, Royal handed me a piece of paper that stated their mission. They wanted it to be "an adventure in building a successful business by doing things that had not been done before." They wanted also to succeed "through the maximum personal growth and creative contribution of each member of the team," everyone working together so that the total was far more than the sum of the parts. The company was more than buying and selling. It was about personal development as well as professional, and improving the communities that the business served. In all of this, a high value was placed on respect among the members of the team and on the enjoyment of each work day. Yet Royal and Liz were currently in an uncomfortable situation of having to dismiss an employee. There were enemies, as with any company, people who had fallen away or who were unfriendly competitors. At no turn was life without its opposition.

As I poked around the store, asking people questions about Royal, Kaitlin Klaussen, who worked in design for Royal and Liz, described Royal to me as "somewhat aloof, his thoughts in the clouds, but very helpful with solutions when a problem was presented to him by employees or friends." This desire to provide strength was one of those guiding principles of Royal's life--but also perhaps was the divine center of his struggles in climbing, kayaking, business, and as a person.

One thread that could be traced throughout Royal's career as a climber was his desire to encourage people to have more confidence in their abilities and to believe in their worth, to set their goals higher. In him, these abilities were practiced. Whether as a designer and seller of clothing, or as an adventure kayaker, or as America's most distinguished rock climber, or as a facilitator for people-building seminars, his was a story of the growth of friends around him as much as the human evolution of one man. At almost every turn, the life of Royal Robbins was strong, positive participation in the lives of people.

He offered the comment that I seemed to hold myself back in certain areas.

Trying on shirts at the store, I noticed an amusingly arrogant ad: "When you think about it, all the important things in life begin with Royal Robbins." I took this as another example of Royal having fun. He loved to compete, but he loved also to have fun. In Modesto, we experienced wonderful periods of laughter. He could see himself as a bit of a fool at times but hoped perhaps that he had also a little of the divine fool.

An elderly gentleman at a gas station said to Royal, "I haven't run out of gas in twenty years, and now I run out." Royal offered the friendly reply, "Makes you feel young again." It was this congenial person of Royal that was, to me, most appealing. He had other sides that at times would return, as though out of the past, for example his old same, disconcerting rigor, where he would gaze at you almost with coldness--a serious and somber fellow, described well by TM Herbert: "If he's not in a communicative mood, he'll sit there and read the paper right in your face."

Yet a few sips of wine in the evening, or a thought of heading off for a few days in the mountains, or the spark of a new idea related to the business, and Royal's sense of humor switched from severe to genial and wise and playfully robust. It was also Herbert's observation: "Some people look at me as if to ask, 'You had a good time with Royal?' But yes some of the best times I've ever had were with Royal, times I'll never forget."

I found Damon to be like Royal--led by his own strong focus. He could shift his attention from you in a second. The same self-determination seemed to act upon the entire Robbins family--being with you in full at an instant of relaxation, then conveying suddenly a feeling that there was another business elsewhere.

There was a lot on Royal's mind. He was high up in a climb, struggling for self-preservation, in their business. He was experiencing the "runouts" of financial responsibility. And the organization required for his business to be a success was partly in the hands of other "belayers" and support team. He was not solo, not able of himself to determine the outcome.

Each day of my visit to Modesto, I would present a chess problem to Damon. He would set his mind to solving it. One evening, I played chess with Royal. He mentioned in a humble way, but with detectable pleasure, that he had briefly been the "first board" player on the Modesto chess club. During our game, Betty snuck her tongue into Royal's glass and lapped up a sip of Burgundy. Her wide-eyed, instantly astonished look gave Royal a chuckle. I wondered if Betty would develop (as a result of her alcohol imbibing) the same slight retention problems Royal had. Upon occasion, he would enthusiastically share with you something he had shared with you the day before. Or he would seem to forget to do something he had said he was going to do.

He did not forget to make the right moves in our chess game, except until just before the end. Managing a clearly winning position and no more than a move or so from mating me, Royal overlooked a cheap mate that I was able to surprise him with. We laughed, and he complimented me for my tenacity. I admired the gracious spirit in which he accepted the undeserved loss.

Royal was aware that not all of life could be victorious. He seemed to have no doubt that challenges, adversity, lay ahead. The apparel business all across the country was in a difficult economic slump, and his company was in need of a new discovery, an uplift, a chess problem-like solution. A few days earlier, Liz had pointed out to me how tenuous a successful business could be, how that if she and Royal were to fail they would "lose everything."

Somehow, I was not afraid for them. Their fate was too charged with their positive commitment to life. A few nights earlier at dinner, Royal spoke about the possibility of a family ascent of El Capitan in February. He said that he was intrigued by the solitude at that time of the year and the added adventure of unknown weather. "The experience would be worth more." Damon asked some shrewd questions about the techniques that would be used. When Royal mentioned "direct-aid," Damon was surprised that they would have to--or that climbers ever had to--use such devices. Royal reminisced to Damon about how, in the early days on El Capitan, they hammered pitons one above the other into cracks and used those pitons to support body weight. Damon replied, "You mean you didn't really climb it? I would rather climb it."

Tamara was intrigued by climbing, and could read books and magazines on the subject for days on end, but did not enjoy doing it. A family story was the screaming terror-fit she had as a little girl in the middle of some climb.

Damon asked if I was going to include him in the biography, and he began providing me with facts about his life: that he once had a seizure and now had to take medication. I learned also that at age six he had climbed the Great White Book in Tuolumne with Royal and was the youngest person to do the route. Damon described himself: "I am very hyper, a pyromaniac, and like paintball guns...." He would soon realize a sincere and thoughtful passion for drawing.

We took an evening walk up the street, as a family. Climbers were, in a sense, family. Royal was glad that his friends of thirty or even forty years ago were still his friends. Having a sense of each other's love and dependability, those friends and he had placed their lives in each other's care through many adventures. Pratt was still elusive, guiding for Exum in the Tetons in summer and living in Thailand in the winter. Frost was a devout Mormon. TM Herbert was still climbing in Yosemite--sometimes with his sport-climber son, Tom. Fitschen was retiring from teaching, about to remarry and move to New York. Royal and Liz had spent an evening with him at the cabin recently.

A few friends were gone now. John Harlin died when his rope broke on the Eiger. Tom Patey rappelled into the sea off the coast of Wales. Gary Hemming shot himself in the Tetons. Mick Burke disappeared on Everest. Don Whillans passed away in his sleep at his house in England, from exhaustion, or pneumonia, after a long motorcycle trip through Europe and the Alps. Sheridan Anderson died young of an acute attack of emphysema. As we walked, I imagined that for Royal to stare into the stars gave him a memory of all his friends, those living and dead, those of earlier days and current. Perhaps the constellations made him think of climbing or brought him quietly again to its expectation.

Liz told me that there were several things that were "typical of Royal," and all were part of his constant awareness of the natural world. He loved to study the constellations. You could count on him to observe the type of cloud formations and to know their significance for coming weather. He wouldn't step outside without saying how or which way the wind was blowing, noticing what it was doing at ground level and above. He loved the botanical names of trees--he knew them all--despite that he could not remember a single name of the flowers in the garden. Royal would explain patiently to a listener that there were two types of redwoods in California, the Sequoia gigantea of the Sierra and the Sequoia sempervirens ("always living") of the coastal mountains. His favorite was the genus, Pseudotsuga, taken from the Greek word pseudo, false, and Tsuga, which is Japanese for hemlock tree, and thus the genus of false-hemlocks. In the U.S., there were two species, Pseudotsuga douglasi, or Douglas-fir, and Pseudotsuga macrocarpa, or Bigcone-Spruce. And these trees were neither spruce nor fir nor hemlock, so there was falseness all around!

As we walked, huge sycamores and maples of the neighborhood blew serenely. The wind coming from the south was, as Royal stated, "a good sign." It was an indication that at last there was going to be some badly needed rain.

When I asked Royal if he would share with me the evolution of his spiritual beliefs, he offered a succinct, powerful answer: "The love of God was pretty much scared out of me early on by the intellectuals and writers, some of them existentialists, who felt that belief in God was a sign of weakness. So it took awhile...to break through to the truth. But it came through to me very forcefully one afternoon in about '83 while kayaking. I was sitting in my boat on the Middle Fork of the Salmon River when I felt the unmistakable presence of God, behind me in the direction of my right shoulder. Since then," he continued, "it has been a matter of knowledge rather than faith. My desire has been to renew that contact and hopefully to have it on a steady, ongoing basis. Then, you would be there."

I later related the details of Royal's spiritual experience to Tom Frost, and Tom said that it was an experience worthy of such a choice spirit. Doug Tompkins had a different opinion: "I worry about Royal, because he is in an unsteady moment in his life."

Royal confided in me that he had a goal: "Whatever danger may come to me or to my loved ones or to the business or to my health, I hope that I will be able to approach it with equanimity and calm." This echoed his North America Wall article, of 1964, in which he had made an almost identical comment. Royal was speaking of accountability. Instead of "man is his own star" in the proud, self-contained sense, it was "man is his own star" depending upon how the blessings of a life were valued.

Royal's definition of growth was adventure, a greater, deeper meaning of the word, and the greatest adventure was to know God. Such seemed to eclipse being stranded high up in the Cyclop's Eye of El Capitan in a storm. Royal pondered the forces within us that create our predicaments and that bring us close to destruction but also that are key to our advance. He quoted a passage from Whitman:

> "Now understand me well--It is provided in the essence of things,
>   that from any fruition of success,
>   no matter what, shall come forth something
>   to make a greater struggle necessary."

Royal took a sip of wine, smiled. He appreciated those words.

It was time for me to leave Modesto. Royal drove me to my train and waited with me for it. We walked out onto the track. He followed the track with his eyes to where it vanished, and he said, "This appeals to me, to get on a train and go off, away, into the distance." I wondered if he was thinking of the freight train riding of his youth. He shook my hand. His forcefulness, his presence, still aroused my care, in all that I thought and said and did.

Later as I looked up the Whitman quote, I noticed another small passage in the same poem:

> "Now I see the secret of the making of the best persons,
> It is to grow in the open air, and to eat and sleep with the earth."

How does one go forward? Feeling, movement, art, risk of life and limb? Courage inexhaustible, spirit, love? And belief too decorates the face of the climber. Suffering, and rushes of memory, their offering. To recognize the value of a life is not easy--whether it be another's or your own. But once this is recognized, all else--in a sense--is found.

For example, granite in the mystical form of a wall. A feeling of great good fortune, the childhood, the happiness, of smooth, bare rock, its solitude, its strength, its roofed edges rising so immediately upward into the blue of the sky. Climbing at the edge of the nerves. After there has been rain, sunlight falls through the clouds from the outside world and comes to remain in the paradise of one's understanding. Fern-filled timber, oaks, maples, sequoia. Starlight. A smell of water, a warm, oceany breeze of summer. Air beautiful, respirable, held in the inner dwelling places of the mind. Treetops full of winds that, as Sheridan Anderson wrote, "have heard all the sounds of the world."

216 Sentinel Rock -- photo by Tom Frost

217 Half Dome -- photo by Harry Daley

218 Sunlight on El Capitan -- photo by Tom Frost

219 Shadow behind El Cap Spire -- photo by Tom Frost

Selected Bibliography of Writings by Royal Robbins

1. Three Firsts At Tahquitz. *The Mugelnoos*, No. 318, June 11, 1959, published by the Sierra Club.
2. A Real Bloodsucker. *The Mugelnoos*, No. 319, July 9, 1959, published by the Sierra Club.
3. Funclimbing In Yosemite. *The Mugelnoos*, No. 322, October 8, 1959, published by the Sierra Club.
4. El Capitan--First Continuous Ascent. *The Mugelnoos*, No. 334, October 13, 1960, published by the Sierra Club.
5. Climbing El Capitan. *Sierra Club Bulletin*, December, 1960, pp. 47-55, published by the Sierra Club.
6. New Climbs In The Grand Tetons. *Sierra Club Bulletin*, October, 1961, pp. 53-54, published by the Sierra Club.
7. The Royal Arches Direct. *Sierra Club Bulletin*, October, 1961, pp. 56-57, published by the Sierra Club.
8. The North Face of Lower Cathedral Rock. *Sierra Club Bulletin*, October, 1961, pp. 57-58, published by the Sierra Club.
9. The Northwest Face of the Higher Cathedral Spire. *Sierra Club Bulletin*, October, 1961, pp. 58-59, published by the Sierra Club.
10. Yosemite's Higher Cathedral Spire. *Summit Magazine*, January, 1962, pp. 10-12.
11. North Wall of Sentinel Rock. *Summit Magazine*, March, 1963, pp. 9-11.
12. A New Route on the Petit Dru. *American Alpine Journal*, 1963, p. 375, published by the American Alpine Club.
13. The Salathe Wall, El Capitan. *American Alpine Journal*, 1963, pp. 332-337, published by the American Alpine Club.
    (This article can also be found in *The Vertical World of Yosemite*, edited by Galen Rowell, published in 1974 by Wilderness Press, Berkeley, California)
14. The East Wall of Upper Yosemite Fall. *American Alpine Journal*, 1964, PP. 75-78, published by the American Alpine Club.
15. The North America Wall. *American Alpine Journal*, 1965, pp. 331-338, published by the American Alpine Club.
    (This article can also be found in *The Vertical World of Yosemite*, edited by Galen Rowell, published in 1974 by Wilderness Press, Berkeley, California)
16. A Visit To Britain. *Summit Magazine*, December, 1966, pp. 5-9.
17. Talus of Yosemite. *Summit Magazine*, June, 1968, p. 33.
18. The West Face--El Capitan. *American Alpine Journal*, 1968, pp. 73-75, published by the American Alpine Club.
19. The West Face of El Capitan. *Ascent Magazine*, 1968, pp. 2-4, edited by Steve Roper and Allen Steck, published by the Sierra Club.

(This article can also be found in *The Best Of Ascent*, edited by Steve Roper and Allen Steck, Sierra Club Books, San Francisco, 1993)

20. Grand Sentinel. *American Alpine Journal*, 1968, pp. 77-80, published by the American Alpine Club.
21. Cutting Canadian Capers. *Summit Magazine*, October, 1968, pp. 14-19.
22. Time For A Change. *Summit Magazine*, November, 1968, pp. 2-5.
23. Alone on the John Muir Wall, El Capitan. *American Alpine Journal*, 1969, pp. 318-322, published by the American Alpine Club.
24. Incident On Half Dome. *Summit Magazine*, January-February, 1969, pp. 2-5.
25. Solo Ascent of El Capitan. *Summit Magazine*, March, 1969, pp. 12-17.
26. An Excursion in Scotland. *The Scottish Mountaineering Club Journal*, 1969.
    (This article can also be found in *Mirrors In The Cliffs*, edited by Jim Perrin, published by Diadem Books Ltd., London, 1983)
27. Californians in Alaska. *American Alpine Journal*, 1970, pp. 58-62, published by the American Alpine Club.
28. Tis-sa-ack. *Ascent Magazine*, 1970, pp. 14-19.
    (This article can also be found in *The Vertical World Of Yosemite*, edited by Galen Rowell, published in 1974 by Wilderness Press, Berkeley, California, and can be found in *The Games Climbers Play*, edited by Ken Wilson, published by Diadem Books Ltd., London, 1978, and in *The Best of Ascent*, edited by Steve Roper and Allen Steck, Sierra Club Books, San Francisco, 1993)
29. Tis-sa-ack. *American Alpine Journal*, 1970, pp. 7-8, published by the American Alpine Club.
30. Scree. *Summit Magazine*, July-August, 1970, p. 36.
31. The Prow. *Summit Magazine*, July-August, 1970, pp. 2-7.
32. Basic Rockcraft. La Siesta Press, California, 1971.
33. Advanced Rockcraft. La Siesta Press, California, 1973.
34. Jack of Diamonds. *CLIMB!*, edited by Bob Godfrey and Dudley Chelton, 1977, pp. 121-124, published by Alpine House, Colorado.
    (This article can also be found in *Mirrors In The Cliffs*, edited by Jim Perrin, published in 1983 by Diadem Books Ltd., London, and can be found in *Beyond The Vertical*, by Layton Kor and Bob Godfrey, published in 1983 by Alpine House, Colorado)
35. A Review Of Downward Bound. *Mountain Gazette*, May, 1975.
    (This article can also be found in *The Games Climbers Play*, edited by Ken Wilson, published in 1978 by Diadem Books Ltd., London)
36. Foreword. *Mirrors In The Cliffs*, pp. 13-15, edited by Jim Perrin, published 1983 by Diadem Books Ltd., London.
37. Foreword. *Beyond The Vertical*, pp. 7-9, by Layton Kor and Bob Godfrey, published in 1983 by Alpine House, Colorado.

38. Foreword. *First Descents--In Search of Wild Rivers*, pp. ix-x, edited by Cameron O'Connor and John Lazenby, published in 1989 by Menasha Ridge Press, Alabama.
39. Sierra Traverse. *First Descents--In Search of Wild Rivers*, pp. 61-67, edited by Cameron O'Connor and John Lazenby, published in 1989 by Menasha Ridge Press, Alabama.
40. A Final Tribute. *The Climbing Cartoons of Sheridan Anderson*, pp. 141-142, text by Joe Kelsey, published in 1989 by Richard DuMais, High Peaks Press.

Other Suggested Readings

1. "Up Against The Walls," by Joe Fitschen, *Ascent Magazine* 1970, published by the Sierra Club.
2. "Interview With Royal Robbins," by Ken Wilson, Allen Steck, and Galen Rowell, in *The Vertical World Of Yosemite*, edited by Galen Rowell, published in 1974 by Wilderness Press, Berkeley, California.
3. "Royal Robbins--Hard Man From Modesto," by John Cleare, in *Mountains*, by John Cleare, published in 1975/6 by Crown, New York.
4. "Man Is His Own Star," by James Salter, *Quest Magazine*, March/April 1978, published by the Ambassador International Cultural Foundation, Pasadena, California.
5. "Robbins--On The Plank," by Pat Ament, in *Mirrors In The Cliffs*, edited by Jim Perrin, published in 1983 by Diadem, England. Also in *High Endeavors*, by Pat Ament, published in 1991 by Mountain N' Air Books, La Crescenta, California.
6. "The Greatest Show On Earth," by Tom Patey, in *One Man's Mountains*, by Tom Patey, published in 1986 by Victor Gollancz Ltd., London.
7. "Hubris," by Edwin Drummond, in *A Dream Of White Horses--Recollections Of A Life On The Rocks*, by Edwin Drummond, published in 1987 by Diadem, England.
8. *The Climbing Cartoons of Sheridan Anderson*, text by Joe Kelsey, published in 1989 by Richard DuMais, High Peaks Press.

Index

LIST OF PHOTOS

303

About the Author

When I first met Pat Ament in Boulder, Colorado, in 1963, he was an eager youth, filled with dreams about climbing, and proud to be a climbing partner of Layton Kor. My wife, Liz, and I were immediately taken by Pat's enthusiasm for climbing and he joined us that summer as we toured the west and climbed everything that caught our sight. He became our life-long friend and continues to amaze me with his own personal growth, the power of his mind, and the depth of his insights. I am also amazed by the breadth of his mastery of disparate disciplines, from chess through karate, drawing, film-making, music (piano), and photography, to the various forms of wordplay, such as biography, essays, and his first love, poetry. Pat runs broad and deep.

A gifted writer, he is a keen and thorough student of the American climbing scene. He has done a first-class job of the biography of our mutual friend, the great American climber, John Gill. I am pleased that Pat has taken on the challenge of explicating your truly in this book. Climbers often hold in their hands the lives of their companions. I have always felt confident with Pat as a climbing partner. Now, in this biography, as then, I know I am in good hands.

—Royal Robbins